ENGLISH

STAINED AND PAINTED

GLASS

KING'S COLLEGE, CAMBRIDGE

The Betrayal, *c.* 1515–17

ENGLISH STAINED AND PAINTED GLASS

BY

CHRISTOPHER WOODFORDE

OXFORD
AT THE CLARENDON PRESS
1954

Oxford University Press, Amen House, London E.C.4
GLASGOW NEW YORK TORONTO MELBOURNE WELLINGTON
BOMBAY CALCUTTA MADRAS KARACHI CAPE TOWN IBADAN
Geoffrey Cumberlege, Publisher to the University

PRINTED IN GREAT BRITAIN
AT THE UNIVERSITY PRESS OXFORD
BY CHARLES BATEY
PRINTER TO THE UNIVERSITY

PREFACE

THIS book is an attempt to give a brief but balanced account of English stained glass from its beginnings to the present day. It is a forerunner of a larger and more detailed work on the same subject. It is also intended to be a stimulus to others to work in a field where so much remains to be done.

As will be seen, stained glass has had its vicissitudes, but has never lost its popularity. As a work of art, a stained-glass window has its limitations. When those limitations have been acknowledged and utilized by the skilled glass-painter in any period, it is an object of great beauty. It would be as foolish to say that all English stained glass produced before the year 1500 is good as to say that all English stained glass produced after the year 1800 is bad. It is equally foolish to believe that a window made during the reign of Queen Victoria is not worth looking at because it was not made in the reign of King Edward I. A window may be odious; but it must be intrinsically odious, not odious by comparison. Furthermore, there are windows which, for one or more reasons, are failures as works of art and aids to devotion. They may offend our artistic and religious sensibilities, but they may be excellent mirrors of their times and, as such, worthy of serious consideration and careful preservation. It is not safe to assume that something which is poison to this generation cannot be meat to a future generation.

Luminosity, colour, design, drawing, and appropriate subject-matter are perhaps the five main ingredients of a successful stained-glass window. Luminosity is only slightly suggested in a monochrome reproduction in a book, and colour not at all. Much is lost; but such reproductions are valuable if they lead people to look at the windows themselves. They are more profitable than such coloured reproductions as are untrue to the originals. A partial knowledge is better than a false impression of the window.

In the pages that follow I have not described the making of a stained-glass window. The best general description of medieval methods and materials is in the chapter entitled 'Glazing' in Mr. L. F. Salzman's *Building in England down to 1540* (Oxford, 1952). Anyone who studies the details of this aspect of stained glass soon discovers how greatly he is indebted to the researches of Mr. J. A. Knowles, a list of whose writings up to the year 1943 will be found in volume ix of the *Journal of the British Society of Master Glass-Painters*. The technique of the twentieth-century glass-painter is described in E. W. Twining's *The Art and Craft of Stained Glass* (London, 1928) and C. W. Whall's *Stained Glass Work* (London, 1931).

The list of works printed on pages 67–69 is intended to be a guide to the reader who wants more detailed information about the principal examples of stained glass mentioned in the text of my book. I have made much use of the *Journal of the British Society of Master Glass-Painters*. It is indispensable to the student of English stained glass and glass-painters, both past and present. I here make a general and grateful acknowledgement of my debt to the contributors to it.

Although it contains many omissions, Philip Nelson's *Ancient Painted Glass in England, 1170–1500* (The Antiquary's Books, 1913) is still the only general guide to ancient glass in this country. It gives, county by county, lists of churches and some other buildings containing pre-Reformation stained glass with succinct descriptions of it. My list of works on stained glass includes several more exhaustive surveys of glass in particular counties and buildings. There are others, such as L. C. Evetts's 'Medieval Painted Glass in Northumberland' in *Archaeologia Aeliana*, Fourth Series, vol. xx. It is essential to consult the well-indexed volumes produced by the Royal Commission on Historical Monuments (England) for those counties so far surveyed. It must be remembered, however, that there is no mention of glass produced after 1714, except in the volumes devoted to the *City of Oxford* (1939), in which later eighteenth-century glass is briefly noticed, and to *West Dorset* (1952), in which the terms of reference have been extended to the year 1850. For modern stained glass reference should be made to *Some Stained Glass Windows Executed within the Past Twenty Years,* issued by the British Society of Master Glass-Painters in 1930, and *A Directory of Stained Glass Windows Executed within the Past Twenty Years*, issued by the same Society in 1939, 1949, and 1952. These publications refer only to the work of the glass-painters who belong to that Society. Further guidance will be found in the Reports of the Central Council for the Care of Churches.

Mr. Laurence Tanner has kindly informed me about the windows made by William and Joshua Price for Westminster Abbey in the eighteenth century. Mr. John Betjeman and Sir Thomas Kendrick have given me invaluable help concerning the early nineteenth-century glass-painters. In the List of Plates will be found the names of those upon whose photographs the plates are based and also those who have given permission for the photographs to be reproduced. I much appreciate their kindness. The photography of stained glass is never easy and is sometimes extremely difficult. In a number of cases the photographers have spared no pains to get the best possible results especially for this book. Amongst those who have helped me to obtain photographs I must mention Mr. Cecil Farthing and Miss Gladys J. Gardner, of the National Buildings Record, Dr. L. A. Hamand, Mr. Dennis King, Mr. J. A. Knowles, the Rev. W. W. Lillie, the Rev. T. W. Keith Murray, Mr. Donald B. Taunton, and the Very Rev. E. Milner-White, Dean of York. I have put them to considerable trouble and they have been most patient with me.

C. W.

OXFORD, 1953

The design on the cover is based upon
the decoration on a
fifteenth-century glazing quarry in
Guilden Morden church, Cambs.

CONTENTS

LIST OF PLATES

II. THE FOURTEENTH CENTURY

III. THE FIFTEENTH CENTURY

IV. THE SIXTEENTH CENTURY

V. THE SEVENTEENTH CENTURY

VI. THE EIGHTEENTH CENTURY

VII. THE NINETEENTH CENTURY

VIII. THE TWENTIETH CENTURY

I

THE TWELFTH AND THIRTEENTH CENTURIES

THE beginnings of glass-painting in England are obscure. It is probable that York Minster contains the earliest glass that could have been produced in England. There is an incomplete panel showing a seated king from a 'Tree of Jesse' which is so like panels in the abbey of St.-Denis and at Chartres that there must have been a common origin at least for the design of the windows. The St.-Denis glass was painted some time between 1142 and 1151 and the Chartres glass about 1145. The York Minster glass is probably more or less contemporary and therefore was not painted, as was once supposed, for the choir built by Archbishop Roger between 1151 and 1181 but for Thomas of Bayeux's church, which was pulled down in 1154. If this date for the panel is accepted, it was made about a century later than the earliest surviving stained glass, which is in Augsburg Cathedral.

Other glass in York Minster is also attributed to the twelfth century, namely, a panel showing the 'Visit of Habbakuk to Daniel in the Lions' Den', now in the central light of the 'Five Sisters' window, and considerable remains of borderwork in the nave clerestory windows; but it is unlikely that this glass is of as early a date as the 'Tree of Jesse' panel.

The outstanding example of glass-painting of this century is the great series of figures in Canterbury Cathedral (Pls. 1, 2). The figures, which represent the descent of Christ from Adam, were set two by two and one above the other in the choir clerestory windows. The series is not now complete and the figures are scattered among various windows of the cathedral. They were produced at various dates between *c.* 1178 and the end of the century.

Other important glass in the cathedral is about contemporary with these figures. There are representations of Moses and the 'Synagogue', of the 'Four Cardinal Virtues' and of the 'Four Major Prophets' in the rose window of the north-east transept. The window in the south-east transept still contains foliage decoration, but no figures remain. A striking representation of the Blessed Virgin Mary and Child within a wide border in the east window of the crypt belongs to the last years of the century.

There is very little glass elsewhere that can be ascribed to the twelfth century. There are a figure and some foliage decoration in the south rose window in Lincoln Cathedral and a head, which may have come from Rochester Cathedral, in the Victoria and Albert Museum. More important is a small window in Brabourne church (Kent) (Pl. 3). It is filled with glass leaded into a purely decorative design. There is little colour; paint is used only to indicate the petals of the rosettes which occur at intervals.

The so-called 'Theological' windows and a good deal more glass in Canterbury Cathedral belong to the turn of the century. The 'Theological' windows, originally twelve in number, were in the choir aisles and the two eastern transepts. They showed a scheme known as 'type and anti-type'; that is to say, a scene from the New Testament ('anti-type') was coupled with one or more scenes from the Old Testament and, occasionally, legends and secular history ('type'), which were supposed to foreshadow it. The scheme became systematized in the *Biblia Pauperum* early in the thirteenth century and in the *Speculum Humanae Salvationis* in later years. Amongst other glass of this date in the cathedral are some roundels now in the three windows of the triforium of the north choir aisle, where they are set against rather later glass (Pl. 4). The design and colouring of some of them are of great beauty. The 'type and anti-type' panels in the east window of the corona were painted about twenty years later. The famous St. Thomas Becket glass in the main aisles of the Trinity chapel was produced during the years 1200–30 (Pl. 5).

The other collection of thirteenth-century glass comparable with that at Canterbury is in Lincoln Cathedral. It is probable that most of it was produced in the first quarter of the century. The great round window in the north transept retains nearly all its glass *in situ*. It portrays the 'Day of Judgement and the Kingdom of Heaven'. An analysis of the other glass, none of which is in its proper place, shows that it represents, often by two or three panels only, the glazing of a considerable number of windows. There were windows showing the 'History of Moses' and 'Illustrations of the Mosaic Law', 'types and anti-types', the 'Parable of the Prodigal Son', the 'Life and Miracles of the Blessed Virgin Mary', the 'Life and Acts' of such saints as John Evangelist, Matthew, Denis, Hugh of Lincoln, and Nicholas.

The lesser collections and single panels and medallions, which are to be found here and there throughout England, mostly belong to the second half of the century. Scenes from the 'Infancy of Christ' remain in a number of churches, such as Aldermaston (Berks.), Ashbourne (Derby.), Doddington (Kent), Lanchester (Dur.), Ledbury (Hereford.), Madley (Hereford.) (Pl. 6), Stragglethorpe (Lincs.), and in the Jerusalem Chamber, Westminster Abbey. The 'Last Supper' is depicted at West Horsley (Surrey), and 'Pentecost' and the 'Ascension' in the Jerusalem Chamber, Westminster Abbey. Part of the famous legend of the Blessed Virgin Mary and Theophilus is shown in panels in Lincoln Cathedral and the church of St. Denys, Walmsgate, York. There are scenes from the life of St. John Evangelist at Madley (Hereford.), and the 'Beheading of St. John Baptist' is preserved in the Jerusalem Chamber, Westminster Abbey. The 'Life and Acts' of St. Ambrose and of St. Nicholas are to be seen in Beverley Minster (Yorks.). There are also remains of 'St. Nicholas' windows in Upper Hardres church (Kent), and in the Jerusalem Chamber, Westminster Abbey. There is a 'St. Catherine' panel at West Horsley (Surrey). Saints directly connected with England are represented by the 'St. Birinus' panels at Dorchester (Oxon.) and the 'St. Edmund, King and Martyr' medallions at Saxlingham Nethergate (Norf.).

There were other ways of filling the windows besides the placing of panels containing figures and scenes on coloured backgrounds.

The 'Tree of Jesse' was a subject which retained its popularity throughout the Middle Ages. It was a pictorial representation of Jesus Christ's maternal descent from Jesse, the father of David. The scriptural basis for it was Isaiah xi. 1 ff., 'And there shall come forth a rod out of the stem of Jesse, and a Branch shall grow out of his roots', &c. The manner in which the subject was represented did not vary greatly throughout the Gothic period. At the bottom of the composition was the recumbent figure of Jesse. From his body rose a vine, whose inner branches enclosed the kingly ancestors of Christ and whose outer branches enclosed the prophets who foretold His coming. The figure culminated in a representation of the Blessed Virgin Mary and Child (the similarity of the words *virga*, rod, and *virgo*, virgin, did not pass unnoticed), or, occasionally, in a rood with the attendant figures of the Blessed Virgin Mary and St. John Evangelist. The 'Tree of Jesse' was frequently represented in English medieval art. It is still to be seen carved in wood and stone, painted in manuscripts and on the walls of churches, and embroidered on copes. It was a favourite subject in stained glass and was generally placed in one of the eastern windows of the church. There are remains of thirteenth-century 'Tree of Jesse' windows at Nackington and Westwell (Kent), in Salisbury Cathedral, and, if the glass is English, in Kidlington church (Oxon.).

There were also windows composed mostly of white glass which was partly painted with foliage and leaded into more or less complicated patterns. The acanthus foliage, derived from Greek art through Roman and Byzantine ornament, was used everywhere during this period. A larger or smaller amount of coloured glass was generally introduced to break the monotony of the window. It is customary to call these windows 'grisaille windows'. From what remains, it can be discerned that the patterns and designs varied from the very simple to the very intricate. Sometimes the designer cleverly conveys the impression that one pattern has been laid upon another. The best examples are to be seen in Lincoln Cathedral and Salisbury Cathedral (Pl. 7), but a number of parish churches, such as Southacre (Norf.), Stockbury (Kent), and Waterperry (Oxon.), can also show good glass of this kind.

Fragments of glass from 'grisaille' windows are still to be found in many churches. The glass in the well-known 'Five Sisters' window in York Minster is still impressive although it is but a shadow of its former self. Another kind of 'grisaille' window was made of diamond-shaped quarries, each quarry being strongly painted with a floral design, which was often set against a cross-hatched background. A linear border, which is generally called strap-work, was painted upon four or, more often, two edges of the quarry, so that, when the quarries were leaded together, the window appeared to be filled with trellis-work. It may be recalled, in this connexion, that in the Middle Ages, many windows, especially in houses, were filled with a wooden trellis against which was stretched linen or paper treated with oil. Glazing quarries of this date are to be seen fairly frequently, but they are seldom in the window for which they were painted and it is not safe to assume that they were necessarily painted for the churches in which they are now preserved. At Fawkham, Upper Hardres, and Westwell, all of which are in Kent, the foliage springs from a little floriated mound at the base of each quarry, a detail of design which suggests the work of one man or, at least, a local fashion.

In 1134 an ordinance of the Cistercian Order laid down that windows were to be glazed with white glass only and were to contain no figures or 'crosses'. Considerable stress has been laid upon this ordinance and it has been seen as one of the main reasons for the prevalence of the 'grisaille' window in the thirteenth century. It seems improbable that the ordinance and the stern principle which lay behind it could have had so much effect on those who were directly or indirectly responsible for the glazing of churches unconnected with the Order. A desire for a reasonable amount of light may have been one cause of such glazing. An insufficient number of glass-painters skilful enough to produce the more elaborate kind of window may have been another. The main motive, however, must have been expense. The windows, which were even more numerous and of ever-increasing size, had to be glazed as quickly as possible. The grander stained glass could be substituted for the 'grisaille' glass when a donor could be found. It was, maybe, the desire to get the windows glazed quickly and yet to give them sufficient colour and interest to satisfy the donor and to fit in with the other decoration and furniture of the church that led to the production of one of the most pleasing of all designs. This was the placing of one or more panels, containing figures, on the 'grisaille' glass in each light of the window. There are good examples of this kind of window in Hereford Cathedral, at Chetwode (Bucks.), and at Stanton Harcourt (Oxon.) (Pl. 3).

In the second half of the thirteenth century there appeared two subjects which were to take a very important place in stained-glass windows in later generations. One was the figure of the donor of the glass and the other was the heraldic shield. In the Burrell Collection at Glasgow there is a kneeling figure of Beatrix of Falkenburg, wife of Richard, Earl of Cornwall, 'King of the Romans'. She died in 1277. It is more than likely that she gave or bequeathed the window in which this representation of herself appeared to the Franciscan church in Oxford where she was buried. The earliest heraldic glass is represented by six shields in the west window of Salisbury Cathedral, by three shields in the windows of the apse of Westminster Abbey, and by the royal arms in Chetwode church (Bucks.). The Salisbury shields were almost certainly painted between 1262 and 1270. The others are of about the same date.

Like the stained glass, the English glass-painter gradually emerges from obscurity. No one can tell whether the earliest windows are English or French. The twelfth-century 'Tree of Jesse' window in York Minster could have been imported from France or painted by Frenchmen who had come to England to execute this and other commissions or painted by Englishmen using French designs and perhaps trained by French glass-painters. There is good reason for thinking that the glass for the eastern clerestory windows in Canterbury Cathedral was designed by Eadwine, a monk of Christ Church, Canterbury, whether it was actually painted by Englishmen or not. Another interesting problem is posed by the titles of the earliest Englishmen who could have been glass-painters, because it is impossible to say with certainty what those titles are intended to convey. A man named *Osbernus vitrarius* witnessed three Ramsey Abbey deeds between 1114 and 1160. Perhaps some light is thrown upon his work by the activities of a monk of Ramsey Abbey, named Daniel, who was contemporary with him. Daniel was said to have been 'pauper vitri tractor et fere laicus'. He was evidently a man of exceptional ability. With the support of King Stephen he supplanted the ruling abbot of Ramsey. He thereafter became abbot of St. Benet-at-Holme in Norfolk, where he remained until he died in 1153. He was a close friend of King Stephen, whose wish that he should become Archbishop of Canterbury was not fulfilled because he could not say mass. It may be that Osberne and Daniel were related or were partners in business before Daniel became a monk. Their business may have been glass-making rather than glass-painting. Stephen, called *Verarius*, sold property in Hemingford, Hunts., in 1198. Hamo, called *Verrarius*, held land of St. Alban's Abbey in 1199. Nicholas, called *Verarius*, appears in a tallage of the city of Canterbury in 1199. It cannot be said whether these men were glaziers or glass-makers. If they were glaziers, another problem arises concerning them and those who came after them. They could have been glass-painters or they could have made simple windows of white glass. It is very improbable that the glaziers could have subsisted on the making of windows of white glass only. It is more reasonable to suppose that all but a very few of them were glass-painters.

The thirteenth century gives more than a dozen names before 1250 and thirty-two between 1250 and 1300. Incomplete as the list undoubtedly is, it probably represents a fair picture of the proportion of the glass-painters working in England in the first and second half of the century. More is known about the Oxford glass-painters than about any of the others. It is evident that they were resident and working in Oxford from the time of King Richard I onwards. They were closely associated with the illuminators (of whom the well-known William de Brailes was almost certainly one), goldsmiths, embroiderers, 'parchminers', and bookbinders.

There were no less than nine glass-painters connected with Westminster. Others were living in such places as Bath, Canterbury, Chester, Chichester, Colchester, King's Lynn, Lewes, Lincoln, and Southwark. Some of them had definite contracts to keep the windows of cathedrals in repair, such as John, *vitrearius*, at Chichester and Nicholas Fayerchild at Norwich.

II

THE FOURTEENTH CENTURY

It was in the fourteenth century that English stained glass reached its greatest beauty of colour and design. The windows of this century also show with what skill and delicacy a glass-painter could paint and pattern his coloured glass without loss of luminosity. Tentative beginnings and crude drawings were left behind: the perfunctory and sometimes weary filling of the vast areas of the later Perpendicular windows were yet to come. Stained glass is essentially a Gothic art and it is in this century that it finds its purest and gayest expression. There are many examples of poor work, but, at its best, it is matchless. There was a rapid progress towards naturalism in the rendering of foliage and towards perspective in the designing of the canopies with their towering battlements, their many pinnacles, their roofs, their traceried windows, and their ribbed vaulting. The figures, even at their most majestic, have a lightness and brilliance never achieved before or afterwards.

At about the beginning of the century an important discovery was made. It was found that white glass could be stained yellow with a derivative of sulphide of silver. The stain, which varied in tone from pale lemon to deep orange, was always applied to the outer surface of the glass. The discovery saved the glass-painter much time and trouble. For instance, it was no longer necessary laboriously to lead a 'pot metal' (glass stained throughout its substance) yellow crown on to a head or 'pot metal' yellow ornaments into a white canopy. Similarly, the decorative patterns and the strap-work on quarries could be stained yellow and the general effect thereby greatly enriched. Judging from the windows in York Minster, where yellow stain was used at a very early date, some glass-painters were quicker than others to seize the opportunities offered by the discovery. It is natural to suppose that the younger men were more ready than their elders to experiment with the stain. In the next century the glass-painters sometimes used two different shades of yellow on one piece of glass to show, for example, pale yellow hair and a golden crown. They also used yellow stain on blue glass to show green objects on a blue background.

Another interesting development was a more skilful and effective method of shading by stippling as well as by smearing on pigment. Also a wider range of colours became available. The new colours were of great beauty and included brown, murrey, violet, and deep green. This glass, like all coloured glass used in England throughout the Middle Ages, came from the Continent.

There are several places in which the development of glass-painting during the first half of the fourteenth century can be studied. It must be emphasized that it is the first of a series of periods for which the glass must be examined in different districts. Although there are characteristics obviously common to all the glass of the period, there are regional differences which are unmistakable. These differences are easier to observe than to describe. A definite impression is made upon the mind, but it is not easily definable in words.

York Minster retains by far the most extensive collection of glass of this date. The windows of the chapter house, the vestibule, the nave aisles and clerestories, and the western windows of the nave were glazed during the first half of the century. There is, moreover, glass which was probably preserved when the choir was rebuilt (Pl. 16). Because the full significance of all this glass is still in process of revelation, it is difficult to pick out salient points. The merest glance round the windows of the nave aisles will show that some of the designers of the windows were attempting, by introducing a double band of coloured panels set on white glass, to counteract rather than to emphasize the perpendicular lines and great height of the building. Much as the glass has suffered in succeeding generations, a general impression of magnificent glazing and a great wealth of iconographical interest remain. The fourteen windows of the nave clerestory each originally included five shields of arms in their glazing. Seventy-six of them remain. It seems probable that they commemorate the gathering of the King's forces at York in 1314 before the campaign against Scotland and the battle of Bannockburn. It is an important example of the early use of heraldic glass on a large scale and according to a definite plan. The 'Tunnoc' or 'Bell-founder' window, made before 1330, the 'Peter de Dene' or 'Heraldic' window, made *c.* 1310, and the 'Penancer's' window, made *c.* 1315–20 (Pl. 10) in the north aisle of the nave, the 'Chancellor's' window, with its scenes from the life and vision of St. John Evangelist, in the south aisle of the nave, and panels in the first window from the west in the same aisle must not escape special mention.

The fourteenth-century glass in Wells Cathedral is some of the most beautiful in England (Pl. 13). When its style is compared with that of contemporary stained glass, it all appears to be the work of a very progressive body of glass-painters. The Lady chapel was glazed *c.* 1300–5: the chapter house, *c.* 1316–18: the chapels of St. John Baptist and St. Stephen, *c.* 1318–22: the choir aisles, *c.* 1320–25: the choir clerestory, *c.* 1325–33: the great east window of the choir, *c.* 1328–34. The figures of ecclesiastics, of kings, and of St. George beneath their tall canopies in the choir clerestory are among the most noble examples of English fourteenth-century glass-painting. The 'Tree of Jesse' in the east window of the choir is one of the great achievements of the period. Its masterly colour scheme is based upon a full use of yellow and vivid greens with cleverly placed patches of red and white glass and with a very sparing use of blue.

The earliest glass in the east window of the choir of Exeter Cathedral was placed in position about the year 1300. The windows of the clerestory and aisles of the choir were glazed during the next eleven years. Not very much of this glass remains, but it is worthy of mention because it is well documented in the fabric rolls which include many items concerning the purchase of glass and the names of some of the men who produced the windows.

The seven windows in the clerestory of the choir of Tewkesbury Abbey were glazed in 1340–4. The east window in the clerestory contains a 'Doom' with the 'Coronation of the Blessed Virgin

Mary' above it. At the bottom of the light is a kneeling nude figure of the donor. She was almost certainly Eleanor de Clare, who married, first, a Despenser and, second, a Zouche. Four other windows contain figures of kings and prophets of the Old Testament, some of them now fragmentary (Pl. 14). In the two westernmost windows there are men in armour representing lords of the manor of Tewkesbury. At the bottom of all the lights are shields of arms, which are still a fine display in spite of the fact that they are not quite complete. These windows repay careful study. Notice may be taken of the tall and elaborate canopies, with their carefully patterned shafts, and of the delicate designs which decorate the coloured backgrounds of the figures. Very skilful use has been made of silvery white glass, of yellow stain, and of a beautiful green to give lightness and brilliance to the windows.

The finest glass-painting of this period is to be seen in the east window of Eaton Bishop church (Hereford.) (Pl. 15). It was probably produced sometime during the years 1317–21. Here design, choice of colour, and richness of decoration all reach a high degree of excellence. It is deplorable that the glass is incomplete, but other more or less contemporary glass in this and adjoining windows shows how far it excels the quite competent work which stands in close conjunction with it. Still more is its beauty realized when it is compared with such uncouth early fourteenth-century glass as remains only a few miles away in the south choir aisle of Hereford Cathedral. The man who painted it certainly painted the glass in the near-by church of Brinsop and the 'Crucifixion' panel in the east window of Mamble church (Worcs.).

The work of one man or one firm is observable in less accomplished work elsewhere. For instance, the representation of the Blessed Virgin Mary and Child at Fladbury and Warndon in Worcestershire (Pl. 17) and of the apostles at Elsing and Saxlingham Nethergate in Norfolk are examples of very closely related local workmanship.

Glass-painting of good quality is shown in a typical panel depicting St. Catherine beneath a canopy at Deerhurst (Glos.) (Pl. 18). It is interesting to compare it with the work of a quite different hand but of about the same date at Arlingham in the same county. The noteworthy windows at Stanford-on-Avon (Northants.), were probably produced just before the middle of the century. It has been suggested that it was painted in Coventry, which was an important centre of glass-painting in the fourteenth and fifteenth centuries.

In the upper part of the three main lights of a window on the north side of the choir of Bristol Cathedral is glass which has not received the attention it deserves. It is considerably restored, but the glass that is original was painted about the year 1320. It shows the martyrdom of St. Edmund. In the middle light is the king bound to a tree and pierced with arrows. Two executioners stand in the outer lights. There are trees behind them and below the feet of each of them is a wolf guarding the head of the martyred king. The figures are set beneath canopies. It will be noticed that the figures do not keep within the niches in which they stand. The whole composition is a clever solution of the problem of spreading a scene over all the lights of a window without sacrificing the essential elements of a successfully designed stained-glass window.

The great east window of Gloucester Cathedral was probably glazed about the year 1350 in memory of the battle of Crécy (Pl. 19). This great Perpendicular window seems to have determined the design of the glass. One writer says that it is 'the first as well as the grandest example of a window filled with tiers of full-length figures, which are so characteristic of the fifteenth century'. Another emphasizes 'the aesthetic triumph of the extensive use of white glass'. A third draws attention to the excellence of the heraldry. It may be questioned if the window deserves such high praise. It might well be argued that there is a poverty of colour and that the use of it is hesitant and faulty. Nevertheless, the window is an important step forward in the development of English glass-painting.

The second half of the fourteenth century is almost as well represented by surviving stained glass as the first half. In the Lincolnshire churches of Barton-on-Humber, Carlton Scroop, Haydor, and Long Sutton there is glass which has so much in common that it may have come from one 'firm'. It was probably produced about the years 1360–80. The very attractive glass in the three northern windows of the Latin chapel in Christ Church, Oxford, was painted about 1365. A panel showing 'St. Anne instructing the Blessed Virgin Mary' in Marsh Baldon church (Oxon.) came from the same 'firm', which was presumably situated in Oxford. About fifteen or twenty years later in date is the remarkable glass at Grappenhall (Ches.). The most important and extensive collection of late fourteenth-century glass is in the ante-chapel of New College, Oxford. It was almost certainly painted in the workshop of Thomas Glazier of Oxford in the years 1380–3. The figures of patriarchs, prophets, apostles, ecclesiastics, and female saints beneath canopies of complicated and varied design deserve careful scrutiny. Parts of the 'Tree of Jesse', which filled the west window, are now in York Minster. The remains of another 'Tree of Jesse' in the chapel of Winchester College (Pls. 20, 21) and three figures of Apostles from the same chapel, which are now in the Victoria and Albert Museum, were produced by Thomas Glazier of Oxford and his assistants between 1393 and 1404. The archaism noticeable in the New College glass is not so apparent in the Winchester College glass.

The design of the stone tracery lights of the fourteenth-century windows was often so intricate that the glass-painters must have been at considerable trouble to fill the lights with stained glass successfully. Their choice usually lay between figure-work, human heads, heraldry, and foliage. It would be difficult to find a more satisfying combination of stonework and figure-work than in the choir aisles of Wells Cathedral, of stonework and heraldry than at Stanford-in-the-Vale (Berks.) and Leasingham (Lincs.), and of stonework and foliage than in Tewkesbury Abbey. The unusual glass in the very elaborate east window of St. Lucy's chapel, Christ Church, Oxford, gives the impression of having been copied from illuminated miniatures. During this period figures of the donors of the glass were sometimes placed in the tracery lights, as at Meldreth (Cambs.), in Wells Cathedral, and in a panel of glass now in the National Gallery at Melbourne, Australia.

The 'Tree of Jesse' occurs in fourteenth-century glass in at least seventeen places and there are records of other examples now lost. Eight of those which survive, namely, in Bristol Cathedral, at Lowick (Northants.), Ludlow (Salop), Madley (Hereford.) (Pl. 6), Mancetter and Merevale (Worcs.), St. Mary's, Shrewsbury, and Tewkesbury Abbey, have so many points in common that it is difficult not to believe that some single and special influence was at work in the production of them. During this century the 'Tree of Jesse' was sometimes, as in Wells Cathedral, at Winchester College, and at New College, Oxford, associated with the 'General Resurrection', which was shown in the tracery lights. A panel of glass in Thaxted church (Essex) shows a member of the Mortimer family, with shield and spear, encircled in a vine stem. It has been suggested that this is the only surviving example of a 'secular' genealogical tree in medieval stained glass. Perhaps a more likely explanation is that at the bottom of a 'Tree of Jesse' window one or more figures of donors were incorporated in the design.

The heraldic glass of this century has already been mentioned several times. There are a number of churches where the care which was bestowed upon its design and enrichment can be appreciated. The shields at Buxhall (Suff.), North Luffenham (Rutld.), Wimpole (Cambs.), and in the chapel of Merton College, Oxford (Pl. 9) are excellent examples. The heraldic border is one of the many kinds of effective borderwork used in the fourteenth century. The golden leopards of England and the golden fleurs-de-lis of France alternating with red and blue glass are often seen, as in the windows of Wells Cathedral. Almost as popular are the castles of Castile and the covered cups of Galicia, first used in reference to Eleanor of Castile, wife of King Edward I. They can be seen in at least a score of churches all over the country. Sometimes the castles are associated with fleurs-de-lis, as at Richard's Castle, Kinsham, and Credenhill in Herefordshire, or with leopards, as at Thorndon (Suff.), or with white quatrefoils, as at Whitchurch (Bucks.), or simply with coloured glass, as at Benington (Herts.). Sometimes the covered cups alternate with coloured glass only, as at Stanford-on-Avon, or with trailing foliage, as at Dronfield (Derby.). Family arms are to be seen as borderwork at Wimpole and at Portbury (Som.).

The remarkable east window of Sellinge church (Kent) was probably painted in the first years of the fourteenth century. The placing of the figures and heraldry in the form of a chevron may be due to the fact that the window commemorates Gilbert de Clare, Earl of Gloucester and Hertford, whose arms included chevronels.

'Grisaille' glass went through interesting stages of development. At the end of the thirteenth century or the beginning of the fourteenth century the trend towards naturalistic representation was exemplified by the glass-painters in a new way. The lights were frequently filled with twining stems springing from a central and thicker stem, the twining stems bearing leaves, flowers, and fruit. Vine, oak, holly, ivy, maple, sycamore, and suchlike are often seen. Sometimes the leading followed the main stems and an irregular or flowing trellis pattern to emphasize and strengthen the whole design (Pls. 11, 12). In other examples the glass was cut into diamond-shaped quarries to make a regular or formal trellis pattern, and the foliage was drawn as if to grow against it. In the chapter house at York, which was glazed about 1300–7, the flowing design was combined with the older geometric pattern. In the interesting series of 'grisaille' windows at Chartham (Kent), which were painted at about the same time as the chapter house windows at York, the transition from the earlier to the later style is also apparent. In Exeter Cathedral the formal patterns were retained and formed a background for heraldic glass, as may be seen in the chapels of St. Mary Magdalene and the Archangel Gabriel.

The new 'grisaille' patterns were usually associated with panels containing single figures or subject-matter. The most notable and probably the earliest example of this kind of glazing is the series of windows in the chapel of Merton College, Oxford (Pl. 8). The windows were glazed some time between 1298 and 1311. The three-light windows contain in each middle light a panel showing a saint beneath a low canopy and flanked, in all but two instances, by kneeling figures of Henry de Mamesfeld, the donor of the glass, in the outer lights. The 'grisaille' glass, which in some windows is of flowing design and in some windows of quarry-work, is relieved by small patches of colour, both in the main and in the tracery lights.

As the century went on the flowing design was abandoned, presumably because it was unnecessarily elaborate and expensive, and quarries only were used. It became the almost invariable custom to enrich the strap-work and some of the trailing pattern with yellow stain. Occasionally the strap-work was further ornamented with patterns painted in black pigment, as at Haydor (Lincs.). Before the end of the century was reached the trailing stems were also abandoned and each quarry contained its own design repeated over and over again. The strap-work was retained for a while, but it also eventually disappeared.

There are many examples of fourteenth-century 'grisaille' glass although there are very few complete windows. Stanton Harcourt (Oxon.) and Bredon (Worcs.) (Pl. 12), both have good windows showing panels set on grisaille. Interesting 'grisaille' patterns are still to be seen at Bloxham and Waterperry (Oxon.), at Hawton (Notts.), in Hereford Cathedral, at Southacre (Norf.), and at Willesborough (Kent). The glass in the chancel windows at Norbury (Derby.) is much decayed, but it still shows with what success trailing foliage and flowing design can be combined with shields of arms. Numberless fourteenth-century quarries remain. When they can be closely examined, as at Edworth (Beds.), North Elmham (Norf.), and Waterperry (Oxon.), the delicacy and dexterity of the painting can be fully appreciated.

The names of a great number of fourteenth-century glass-painters are known. The London glass-painters petitioned for ordinances for their 'mistery' in 1364–5, and from 1368 onwards they had had their two 'masters' or 'wardens', whose appointment is recorded at intervals during succeeding years. The ordinances of the York glass-painters belong to the late fourteenth century. Sometimes, as in the case of John Brampton of London, whose name first appears in 1349 and who died some time between 1383 and 1387, a fairly full and clear picture of the fourteenth-century glass-painters' work and background can be made from various records. As is to be expected, the glass-painters were most numerous in big towns like London, Norwich, and York. They also lived in smaller towns and villages. For instance, there was a flourishing and evidently well-to-do family of glass-painters at Lenton in Nottinghamshire.

The years 1351–2 are important in the history of English glass-painting because of two glazing-accounts which give much detailed information not only about the processes and costs of glass-painting at this time but also about the glass-painters. One account concerns the glazing of the new chapel of St. Stephen, Westminster. The other concerns the glazing of the chapel of St. Edmund and the newly built chapter house of St. George at Windsor Castle. Unfortunately, detailed accounts for the first part of the St. Stephen's chapel work are lost, but it is clear that the glass-painters had begun their work by about the end of 1349. In 1350 John de Lincoln, master of the glaziers for the works in the chapel at Westminster, was appointed to collect as many glaziers and other workmen as were required to complete the work. His commission ranged over twenty-seven counties. A similar order was issued to John Brampton and John de Geddyng a year later. Forty-one men were impressed for the making of the St. Stephen's chapel windows. Some did not stay for the whole period and some were impressed later. Twenty of them stayed on to help with the glass for the windows at Windsor and thirteen other men were impressed to help them. It is possible to trace many of them, such as the Lenton family, John Halstead, William Hereford, and Simon Lynn, back to their native places, where they are generally described by their trade names in the records of the time.

In the thirteenth century and the first part of the fourteenth century 'le verrer' was the title usually applied to the glazier and glass-painter. At York it survived until 1360. The next title was 'glasswright', a word spelt in many ways. It is impossible to say when it ceased to be used because it survived as a surname. It was not commonly used for a glass-painter after the end of the century. The title 'glazier' occurs as early as 1305. Eventually it became the usual descriptive title.

It is rarely possible to connect a glazier with surviving stained glass. As has been said, Thomas Glazier of Oxford was almost certainly responsible for the glass at New College, Oxford. He dined in hall there in August 1386, and continued to do so regularly, though less and less frequently, in succeeding years. He put a picture of himself at the bottom of the 'Tree of Jesse' at Winchester College with the words *Thōms. op̄ator. isti'. vitri.* In 1389–90 the original six-light east window of the choir in Exeter Cathedral was replaced by the present window. Robert Lyen of Exeter contracted with the Dean and Chapter to glaze it partly by adapting the original glass and partly with glass of his own painting. As it now stands, the window contains glass coeval with the first window, glass painted by Lyen in a purposely old-fashioned style, and glass brought, perhaps during an eighteenth-century restoration, from elsewhere.

In 1393 Richard Savage was appointed 'King's Glazier' for life. Similar appointments were made in the following centuries, but it is difficult to decide how long the office had been in existence before Savage's time. It has been said that it goes back to 1240 and that it was then held by a glass-painter named Edward. In 1297 William of Kent succeeded a glass-painter named Robert in what seems to have been much the same office as Richard Savage was to hold nearly a century later. The names of other men have been suggested as holding the office in the thirteenth and fourteenth centuries, but it is by no means clear that they held more than temporary commissions to do the king's work in particular buildings.

III

THE FIFTEENTH CENTURY

CONSIDERING the fifteenth century as a whole, certain generalizations may be made. It is possible to identify regional peculiarities of style. There is a far wider divergence than before between the best and the worst glass-painting, especially in the second half of the century. In some parts of England, especially in East Anglia (Pls. 31, 32, 35), vigorous designing and excellent technique were maintained up to the time of the Reformation. Nevertheless, the main interest of the stained glass of this period lies in the subject-matter. A poorly conceived and badly executed window is often of considerable iconographical interest because it illustrates the religious impulses and devotional fashions of the time. The artistic spirit may have been slackening, but the religious spirit was seeking new means of expression.

Some of the more noble and extensive examples of fifteenth-century glass-painting can be fairly accurately dated. In 1405 John Thornton of Coventry contracted to glaze the great east window of York Minster. In 1408 he had completed, signed, and dated it. The main lights contain, in the upper part, Old Testament scenes from the 'Creation of the World' to the 'Death of Absalom', in the middle part, scenes from the Apocalypse (Pl. 22), and, in the lower part, figures of kings and ecclesiastics. Two other vast windows in the Minster are devoted to St. William of York and St. Cuthbert of Durham. The 'St. William' window was painted about 1422 (Pl. 23); the 'St. Cuthbert' window is a little later. The Minster and many of the parish churches possess a wealth of glass painted during this century. Nearly all of it bears the unmistakable stamp of York glass-painting while at the same time exhibiting varying degrees of skill.

Great Malvern priory church contains more stained glass of this period than any other building in the country. The glass was inserted in the following order: great east window, *c.* 1440 (Pl. 25): choir clerestories, *c.* 1440–80 (Pl. 26): choir aisles, *c.* 1450–75: nave and aisles, *c.* 1480–90: north transept, before 1501. The eastern part of the church gives a good idea of the general effect of a sizeable English church glazed with fifteenth-century glass, which includes large figures and smaller panels showing scenes. A closer examination of the glass shows that many hands were at work upon the windows and that some of them were more competent than others.

The four eastern windows in the ante-chapel at All Souls College, Oxford, were glazed in 1440–1 by John Glazier of Oxford with figures of the Apostles and other saints beneath canopies. They are a good example of this kind of glass, although the representation of the saints, especially the female saints, tends towards the sweet and sentimental. It is not unlikely that the glass now in three other windows of the ante-chapel, but once in the old library, was painted in the workshop of John Prudde, the King's Glazier. The college paid his servant 10*s.* 8*d.* at the end of 1441. Be that as it may, John Prudde certainly glazed the windows of the Beauchamp chapel, Warwick (Pl 27). The contract, dated 1447, survived. The Beauchamp chapel glass is an example of the most costly window that a fifteenth-century English glass-painter could produce. No trouble and no expense were spared to obtain the best available glass and every known method, such as inserting coloured glass 'jewels' into the borders of the robes, was used to give the most splendid effect possible. When all the windows were still full of Prudde's glass and when the other decoration of the chapel was bright and newly painted, the splendid effigy of Richard Beauchamp, Earl of Warwick, on its equally splendid tomb must have seemed to lie in a great casket of almost unbelievable richness.

Another collection of glass which has a brilliance almost equal to that in the Beauchamp chapel is in the chapel and audit chamber of Browne's Hospital at Stamford. This 'Hospital of St. Mary and All Saints' was founded by William Browne, a draper of Stamford. The glass must have been painted in about 1485. The man who painted it undoubtedly produced the beautiful glass in Ayston church (Rutld).

Some of the differences between the windows in various parts of England are clear enough. For instance, the windows of the Norwich glass-painters and of the Somerset glass-painters are as different from each other as they are from the windows of the York glass-painters. A figure or even a head only is so peculiar to one area that it could not be attributed to another (Pls. 23, 35). Sometimes, as in the case of the Somerset and Devon glass-painters, the differences are rather more subtle, but they are evident once an intimate knowledge of the glass has been acquired. For instance, there is a general 'West Country' similarity between the glass at Langport (Som.) and Bampton (Devon) but the differences are unmistakable. The glass of what may be called the mid-western counties is equally distinctive. The 'jewelled' borders of robes, whether suggested by pieces of coloured glass leaded in or simply by outlines in black pigment on yellow stain, are found much more often in Gloucestershire, Warwickshire, and Worcestershire than elsewhere. The crowns worn by kings, queens, and royal saints in the glass at such places as Great Malvern and Hereford Cathedral are more elaborate than those to be seen in most other regions. In the same area, the churches of Bledington and Cirencester (Glos.), Cherington and Wolverton (Warwick.), and Holt (Worcs.) contain glass which shows that the glass-painters of that district liked to put very bold patterns, suggestive of arras hangings, behind their figures. Within such an area it is sometimes possible to see not only a 'regional similarity' but also, now and then, the markedly characteristic work of a single hand or firm, as in the case of the remarkable canopies at Buckland (Glos.) and Coughton (Warwick.).

One way of distinguishing between these local 'schools', if such a word may be used, is to notice the patterns painted upon the quarries (Pls. 28, 40). A great variety of subjects were used to decorate these quarries. Birds were constantly portrayed, sometimes following their own pursuits such as preening themselves and eating worms and beetles, sometimes doing the work of animals, such as drawing a harrow, sometimes engaged upon human activities, such as ringing a bell or drawing ale from a barrel. Family badges, initial letters, rebuses on the names of the donors of the glass, flowers, plants, and such like are often to be found. Nevertheless, most quarries were painted with formal patterns. A few of these patterns, sometimes of an intricate design, mysteriously spread all over England. Others were confined to a single area, such as Cambridgeshire, Norfolk, and Somerset.

Once the characteristics of the glass-painters of a particular region are known, it is possible to see how the glass-painters of that region were asked to supply windows for places outside it. For example, at Buckden (Hunts.) there is glass which was obviously painted by a man living or trained in Norwich, while a mile or two away at Diddington (Pl. 30) there is interesting glass which is quite unlike it and which may have been painted locally. Farther away in the same county, at Wistow, is rather earlier glass which is different from that at Buckden and Diddington. Again, there is glass which has some of the characteristics of the district but which has other details foreign to it. There is a good example of this at Long Melford (Suff.) (Pl. 31). The great series of figures of the Clopton family and their relations are mostly typical of Norwich workmanship, whereas some of the other figures, with their settings, appear to be of the same origin, but with marked differences. Such cases may indicate the calling in of a man from some other district to help with the designing of the windows.

The subject-matter of English fifteenth-century glass can be fairly easily classified. The 'Infancy and Passion of Jesus Christ' is represented by such windows as those at St. Peter Mancroft, Norwich, East Harling (Norf.) (Pl. 32), and Childrey (Berks.). At the time of their painting they may have been seen by some people rather as the 'Joys and Sorrows of the Blessed Virgin Mary', although scenes from the 'Fall of Man', such as those remaining at Horspath (Oxon.), Martham and Mulbarton (Norf.), and Thaxted (Essex) show that the earlier conception was not forgotten. The lives of the great saints of Christendom survive, in a more or less complete or restored condition, in various places. There are, for instance, the 'St. Helena' window at Ashton-under-Lyne and the 'Invention of the Holy Cross' window at Morley (Derby.); the 'St. Catherine' panels at Clavering (Essex) and Hessett (Suff.); the 'St. Margaret' windows at North Tuddenham (Norf.) and Combs (Suff.); the much restored 'St. Laurence' window at Ludlow; the 'St. Martin' panels which were in the west window of the church of St. Martin-le-Grand, Coney Street, York, until the last war (Pl. 24), and the 'St. Thomas Becket' glass at Nettlestead (Kent). The more local saints are represented by the 'St. Robert of Knaresborough' window at Morley (Derby.) and by the great 'St. Cuthbert' and 'St. William' windows in York Minster. There are slighter remains in a number of churches and records of many others which have completely disappeared.

These 'narrative' windows can never have been as numerous as windows containing single figures of saints beneath canopies. For one thing, they must have cost far more to produce, especially as the windows became larger and larger with the passing of the years. Furthermore, the size of the windows made the small panels with scenes artistically inappropriate, although, judging from the great east window and the 'St. Cuthbert' and 'St. William' windows in York Minster, this may not have weighed much with the donor and designer of the windows. Another and much more important factor was the heavenly help which the donor expected to receive in return for his gift. If he paid for a window in honour of St. Laurence, after whom he was probably named at his baptism, he would expect St. Laurence to intercede for him. If he paid for a window containing the figures of a number of saints, he would expect to benefit from the intercessions of them all. A woman might offer a window showing the 'Annunciation' and the 'Coronation of the Blessed Virgin Mary', with attendant angels, in the tracery lights and figures of St. Margaret, to assist her in the perils of child-birth, of St. Barbara, to save her from the perils of thunder and lightning, and of St. Apollonia, to save her from the pains of toothache, in the main lights.

All such figures were votive. In the fifteenth century the subject-matter in the windows, as in the contemporary wall-paintings, was sometimes didactic. New subjects appeared, such as the 'Te Deum', which occurs at York, East Harling and elsewhere, the 'Ten Commandments', as at Ludlow, and, more frequently, the 'Seven Sacraments' and the 'Seven Corporal Acts of Mercy' (Pl. 33). A most unusual window in All Saints', North Street, York, illustrates the 'Pains and Terrors of the Last Fifteen Days of the World' (Pl. 34). The scenes, with their accompanying texts, are based upon 'The Prykke of Conscience', written by Richard Rolle of Hampole in the early years of the fourteenth century. At Long Melford (Suff.), there seems to have been a window extolling and perhaps illustrating the practice of almsgiving. All that now remains of it are pieces of texts, such as (*Quoniam elimosina ab omni peccato et a morte*) *liberat* (*et non patietur animam*) *ire ī tenebras* (Tobit iv. 10, 'Because that alms do deliver from death, and suffer not to come into darkness') and *Cū facis elimosinā noli tuba cane*(*re*) *ante te* (St. Matthew vi. 2, 'When thou doest thine alms, sound not a trumpet before thee'). Most of a window showing the appalling results of swearing by the various parts of God's Body was still to be seen in Heydon church (Norf.). None of it remains, but it is possible to get a very fair picture of what it was like from the eighteenth-century descriptions of it, from early fifteenth-century wall-paintings at Broughton (Bucks.) and Corby (Lincs.), and from other sources.

A renewed devotion to the passion of Christ and an intensified devotion to 'Corpus Christi' resulted in constant representations of the 'Instruments of the Passion' and the 'Sacred Wounds', which were often shown upon shields in the tracery lights. The 'Tree of Jesse' continued to be represented, but perhaps less often than in earlier centuries. There are remains of at least nine such windows, including interesting examples at Barkway (Herts.), Leverington (Cambs.), and Margaretting (Essex). The most remarkable is at Dorchester (Oxon.), where the stonework of the window is incorporated in the design.

Heraldry lost none of its popularity. Merchants' marks remain in the windows of a number of churches, as at Holme-by-Newark and Newark (Notts.), Monks Risborough (Bucks.), and St.

Andrew's, Norwich. There seems to be no surviving stained-glass merchant's mark of the fourteenth century, but the 'Creed' (*c.* 1394), formerly attributed to 'Piers Plowman', in describing a Dominican church, speaks of

> Wyde wyndowes y-wrought· y-written full thikke,
> Schynen with schapen scheldes· to schewen aboute,
> With merkes of marchauntes· y-medled bytwene,
> Mo than twenty and two· twyes-noumbred.

As far as church windows are concerned, in this century the shields were shown in the tracery lights more often than in the main lights. They are frequently held by angels, who either grasp the shields by their edges or hold them by their straps. Sometimes, as at Ashton (Devon), Petrockstow (Devon), and Spexhall (Suff.) the shields hang by their straps from trees. At Eyworth (Beds.), Great Burstead (Essex), and Hildersham (Cambs.) they hang from hooks. At Chilham (Kent) the strap is held by a hand.

Surviving records show that the principal apartments in important secular buildings, such as the royal castles and palaces, had stained glass in their windows at least as early as the first half of the thirteenth century. There was probably more stained glass in the windows of dwelling houses and the domestic parts of monastic establishments than has been generally realized. Nevertheless, the windows of buildings other than churches were glazed with stained glass with increasing frequency as the Middle Ages drew to a close. Private dwelling houses, when built largely of timber, were liable to be burnt down. They were also liable to be partly or wholly rebuilt according to changing architectural fashion, especially those houses which belonged to wealthy men. In the Middle Ages and long afterwards windows were movable possessions liable to be packed away when the family was not in residence and taken away if the house was sold. All these factors made for the loss and destruction of domestic stained glass. A surprising amount remains, although it may not be in the house for which it was painted. The glass which survives and the records of what is lost probably give a fair picture of the kind of stained glass that decorated the later medieval houses. Heraldic glass was much the most frequently seen. The finest and the best designed is that in the hall of Ockwells Manor (Berks.). Each light contains one 'achievement' set upon a background of flowered quarries across which strips of glass are set diagonally. The strips are painted with the motto *ffeyth. fully. serve.* Sacred subjects were to be seen in the windows of houses and of the Oxford and Cambridge colleges. A large collection of roundels of this kind from a house in High-cross Street, Leicester, are now in the Museum in that town. They show, amongst other subjects, the 'Life of the Blessed Virgin Mary' (Pl. 29), the 'Joys of the Blessed Virgin Mary', the 'Seven Sacraments', and the 'Seven Corporal Acts of Mercy'. As Chaucer shows, secular subjects were to be seen in the windows of houses in the fourteenth century. The most popular secular subject in the following century was a series of the 'Twelve Labours of the Months' painted upon roundels. A number of incomplete sets remain, although they have mostly found their way into churches and public and private collections. Excellent examples, from various places, can be seen in the Victoria and Albert Museum (Pl. 29). The 'Nine Worthy Conquerors', usually represented by three pagans, three Jews, and three Christians, such as Hector, Alexander, Julius Caesar, David, Judas Maccabaeus, Josephus, Arthur, Charlemagne, Godfrey de Bouillon, were sometimes shown, as in glass once in a Norwich house and now partly preserved in a private collection.

Some of the quarries now to be seen in churches were doubtless once in houses and inns. Such quarries are preserved in Yarnton church (Oxon.). One shows an owl with a bell and a scroll inscribed *Ye schal praye for ye fox*, which must refer to some version of the famous romance of Reynard the Fox. Another shows a bird with keys hanging from a cord round its body and a pannikin in one of its claws. Its scroll is inscribed *who blamyth this ale*. Four other birds carry scrolls inscribed as follows:

Make the pour to pray wele
Be still or ellis say wele
and make god thy frende
at thy last ende

Interesting subjects now lost were the ancient games of 'cock-shying' and 'barley brake' once depicted on quarries in the window of a house at Farley in the parish of Backwell (Som.) and 'the whole order of plantyng, prugning, stamping, and pressing of vines' in a house called Chilwell, near Nottingham.

There are a number of proverbs and aphorisms like those associated with the Yarnton birds. One set, now divided between the churches of Langley and Thurton in Norfolk, is of fifteenth-century date. A roundel in the town hall at Axbridge (Som.) shows the Holy Dove descending in a glory and the inscription

God that ys lord of all
Save the counseyl of this hall

Not so much is known about the fifteenth-century glass-painters as about those of the fourteenth century. There are many names, but in nearly all cases they remain but names. It is only at York that it is possible to discern a picture of a certain number of families who kept the craft almost entirely in their own hands. Even in that city, where so much information about them has been carefully collected and where so much of their work is still to be seen, it is seldom possible to say which man or firm painted which windows. They received new ordinances in 1463–4 and the London 'Mistery of Glasyers' petitioned for new ordinances in 1474.

Very occasionally, as in the case of John Thornton and John Prudde, it is possible to associate glass-painters with surviving glass. There is another example at Tattershall (Lincs.). In 1482 payments were made to a number of glass-painters who had painted windows for the great collegiate church. They were Robert Power of Burton-on-Trent, John Glazier of Stamford, John Wymonsdeswalde of Peterborough, and Thomas Wodshawe and Richard Twygge who worked in partnership to make a window showing the 'Seven Sacraments' and two other windows showing figures under canopies. Part of the 'Seven Sacraments' window can still be seen. In 1509–10 Richard Twygge was paid for much work done in Westminster Abbey.

The office of King's Glazier is more clearly defined in this century. Roger Gloucester of London was granted the office in 1412. He was succeeded by John Prudde in 1440. There are many records of Prudde's work, but the Beauchamp chapel glass is all that can be definitely attributed to him. He was followed by Thomas Bye of London in 1461. Bye died in the spring of 1472. William Neve was appointed in 1476 and the appointment was renewed in 1485.

It is very likely that the glass in the lower part of the great north window in the north-west transept of Canterbury Cathedral came from the workshop of William Neve (Pl. 37). The window was probably given to the cathedral by King Edward IV in 1482. Very similar to it and presumably of the same origin is glass showing figures of the kings of England in St. Mary's Hall, Coventry, figures in the chapel of Christ's College, Cambridge, and glass in the apse of Westminster Abbey.

IV

THE SIXTEENTH CENTURY

TWO events of importance in the history of English glass-painting occurred in this century. The introduction of glass-painters from Germany and the Netherlands into this country brought a new spirit as well as a new style to the stained-glass window. Before this new spirit and style could have any effect on English glass-painting as a whole the Reformation brought the representation of religious subjects to an end. These two events must be noticed in detail, but attention must first be drawn to some of the glass produced by English glass-painters in the traditional style during the first part of the century.

The windows of St. Neot's church (Corn.) were drastically restored by J. P. Hedgeland soon after 1825; nevertheless they are the most important example of the glazing of a remote church between 1480 and 1530. The windows showing the 'Creation' (Pl. 36) and the stories of Adam, Noah, and St. George are the earliest in the church. Efforts were made to persuade the local gentry to glaze other windows in the church. Then, when the north aisle was widened or rebuilt in the second quarter of the sixteenth century, the whole parish and sections of the parish glazed its windows: thus in 1523 'the wives of the western part of the parish' gave a window with figures of the risen Christ, 'our Lady of Pity', St. Mabena, and St. Maberedus, and 'the young men of the parish' gave the 'St. Neot' window at the same time or a little later. It is possible to detect a deterioration in the drawing and design of the windows during the half century in which they were being produced. It is also to be remembered that they were all probably produced more or less locally. Some of the glass in the church is certainly local work and is exactly like glass in neighbouring churches.

Another interesting window was put up in Greystoke church

(Cumb.) in 1520. It shows the adventures of St. Matthew and St. Andrew in Wrondon, the City of Dogs. The descriptive sentences which accompany the scenes are in English like those in the 'St. Robert of Knaresborough' window at Morley.

The largest single window of glass of this period is the 'Magnificat' window in the transept of Great Malvern priory church. There is good reason to think that it was given to the church by King Henry VII and placed in position in 1501. It is not a success. In the upper part, the great vesica enclosing the scene of the 'Coronation of the Blessed Virgin Mary' covers three of the six main lights and the figure of the Blessed Virgin has to be shown out of the middle line of the window. The scenes, which include eleven 'Joys of Mary', with corresponding sentences from the 'Magnificat' and *Gaude* sentences, are ill-drawn. In some ways this window resembles the 'Royal' window at Canterbury, but it is a feeble and distorted echo of it. The man or firm which painted this window may have painted the glass in the east window of Little Malvern church some years earlier. While speaking of 'Royal' windows mention must be made of the large named figures of King Henry VII and his Queen and the gigantic representation of the royal arms with supporters in the east window of Stanford-on-Avon church. The glass appears to be local work, but it is decorative and effective.

There is a considerable amount of glass which shows the last flickerings of the purely Gothic tradition of design. The panels showing Christ on the cross flanked by the Blessed Virgin Mary and St. John, once in the chapel of Bramhall Hall (Ches.) and now in the Victoria and Albert Museum, is representative of it (Pl. 39). Some examples are dated. There are, for instance, the remains of figures of St. Christopher, of St. Stephen, and of a king or an emperor with attendants, with part of an inscription, *yere of ov^{r} lorde god 1536*, at Barley (Herts.). No colour is used except yellow stain. At Broadwood Kelly (Devon) there is glass which includes figures of the Blessed Virgin Mary from a scene of the Crucifixion, of St. Sitha, and of donors with part of an inscription which includes the date 1523. There is a kneeling priest and the date 1522 in St. Peter Hungate, Norwich.

The quarries were decorated in the traditional way, either with floral decoration or with badges, the royal badges and initials being of special interest. There is an unusual set in Brandeston church (Suff.), where there is also early sixteenth-century figure-work. One quarry shows a pomegranate, the badge of Catherine of Aragon, with the text *Quod deus conjunxit homo non separet* in an abbreviated form on a scroll above it. There are other quarries, bearing royal devices, in the side chapels of the chapel of King's College, Cambridge, in the Victoria and Albert Museum (Pl. 40), and elsewhere. In York Minster there are quarries, said to have been painted between 1502 and 1507, which show a man birching a boy, a performing bear, a man playing several instruments at once, and birds.

A much higher standard was maintained in the drawing of heraldry than of figures. Representations of the royal arms and badges are particularly good. Examples may be seen at Aldermaston (Berks.), Bradenham (Bucks.), and at St. Peter Mancroft, Norwich, in Canterbury Cathedral, in the cloisters of Gloucester Cathedral (from Pricknash Park, Glos.), in the chapel of King's College, Cambridge, and in the Victoria and Albert Museum (from Cowick Priory, Devon) (Pl. 46).

Alongside the purely Gothic and traditional work there was developing a more pictorial window. One of the earliest manifestations of it is in the windows showing the Apostles in Ludlow church (Pl. 38). These windows, which are attractive both in colouring and design, are allied to contemporary but more traditional windows in the church. By far the most important manifestation of this development is the great series of windows in Fairford church (Glos.) (Pl. 41). Yet most of the Fairford windows are disappointing. They are badly painted and many of them are uninspired and lifeless. Some of the best work will be found in the figures of prophets in the nave aisle windows and in the figures in the north clerestory windows, where startling and vicious devils stand above the persecutors of the Church. The Fairford glass is important, not as good glass-painting but as a fortunate survival which shows how a rich man glazed a large church between 1495 and 1505 with glass of more 'up-to-date' design than that at St. Neot. The growing influence of the painted picture and of artistic development in the Low Countries is shown in other glass besides that at Fairford. There is, for instance, the glass in the twenty-one lights of the east window of the chapel of Hengrave Hall (Suff.). The glass, which must have been painted about 1535–8, shows subjects ranging from the 'Creation of the World' to the 'Destruction of Sodom and Gomorrah' and from the 'Annunciation' to the 'Last Judgement'. Here, as at Fairford, the inclusion of smaller scenes in a panel which depicts one large subject can be seen. Thus, the panel which has a large scene of the 'Entry into Jerusalem' contains also the 'Temptation of Christ' and the 'Raising of Lazarus'. The east window of the chapel of Balliol College, Oxford, contains glass presented by Lawrence Stubbs in 1529. It shows the 'Passion, Resurrection, and Ascension of Christ', together with figures of the donor and others. Most attractive glass designed in a quite different style is to be seen in Hillesden church (Bucks.). The east window of the south transept contains eight miracles of St. Nicholas with descriptive texts in Latin, and another text which shows that scenes from his life were also depicted. Other windows in the church have remains of glass of the same character and date. The influence of the new pictorial fashion on the representation of single figures of saints is shown in some of the windows of the chapel of The Queen's College, Oxford. They are dated 1518. The designer has altogether dispensed with canopies. The figures stand against a distant landscape with the sky above them. Their names are boldly written above their heads. Unfortunately, the glass has been repaired and re-set in later years, so that the original effect has been partly lost. The beautiful figure of Anne Shelton in Shelton church (Norf.) (Pl. 42), shows how a donor could be depicted at this time.

There were a few foreign glass-painters in England in the fourteenth century and the first part of the fifteenth century, but, judging from the glass that survives, they had no effect on the general development of English glass-painting. At the end of the fifteenth century others began to settle in England. It is clear enough that a great deal of the glass mentioned above, such as that at Fairford, Hengrave, and Hillesden, owes much to Germany and the Low Countries, but it is impossible to say exactly through what medium the influence made itself felt. It is possible that some of the glass was painted by foreigners, but it is much more likely that it was painted by Englishmen using foreign designs, more or less directly, as a basis for their cartoons.

The windows of the chapel of King's College, Cambridge (Frontispiece and pl. 43), and the contemporary documents which concern their production offer a clearer picture of what was happening at this time. Four of the windows were glazed by Barnard Flower between 1515 and 1517. Flower had come from Germany or the Netherlands. He was at work in England in 1496 and was appointed King's Glazier in or before 1505. He died in 1517. In his four windows there are four panels which are more Gothic in style than the rest and which are very like some of the Fairford glass. After a lapse of nine years, by a contract dated 30 April 1526, Galyon Hone, Richard Bownde, Thomas Reve, and James Nicholson undertook to glaze eighteen windows, and by a contract dated 3 May 1526 Francis Williamson and Symond Symondes undertook to glaze four windows. The great west window, which was included in the contract of Galyon Hone and his fellows, and half one of the other windows were not glazed until recent times. Galyon Hone was a native of Holland and came to England sometime before 1517. He became King's Glazier; the date of his appointment is uncertain. He probably died about 1552. Richard Bownde and Thomas Reve were London glass-painters. James Nicholson came from Germany or the Netherlands. Francis Williamson also came from overseas. Symond Symondes was probably an Englishman. The east window of the chapel contains six scenes from Christ's Passion. Two windows are devoted to apocryphal incidents in the early life of the Blessed Virgin Mary. Three windows contain scenes from the Acts of the Apostles. The rest of the windows are set out on the 'type and anti-type' plan, the Old Testament and other 'types' in the upper lights and the New Testament 'anti-types' in the lower lights. The designer of much of the glass is said to be Dirick Vellert of Antwerp, who was a renowned glass-painter. The scenes in the windows vary greatly in quality as well as design. The Renaissance style is much more evident in some than in others.

There is other glass in England which shows the early influence of the Renaissance. Perhaps the most striking is in Withcote church (Leics.) (Pl. 45). There are prophets with messianic texts, Apostles with sentences from their creed, and royal badges and heraldry. The glass must have been painted in 1537. The chapel of The Vyne in Hampshire contains windows painted about sixteen years earlier than the Withcote glass. It is thought that they are the work of a group of itinerant glass-painters engaged in Calais by Lord Sandys, the builder of the house. The figures of the Blessed Virgin Mary, St. John Evangelist, and St. Mary Magdalene beneath canopies at Temple Guiting (Glos.), show Renaissance details. So does a remarkable window on the north side of the chancel of Winscombe church (Som.) (Pl. 44). It was given by Peter Carslegh, vicar of Winscombe 1521–32, and shows three of his 'name saints', Peter the Apostle, Peter the Deacon, and Peter the Exorcist. The whole window is done in white glass, black pigment, and yellow stain. When this window is compared with the late fifteenth-century windows in the church, it will be seen that, despite its Renaissance features, it is in the direct line of succession from them.

There were many English glass-painters working in England in the first part of the sixteenth century. The glazing of Little Saxham Hall, near Bury St. Edmunds, is a good example of this. The building of the Hall was begun about 1505. Several men were called upon to glaze the windows. William Duxfold of London and John Glazier of Colchester did part of it. Robert Beston of Bury St. Edmunds painted imagery and heraldry. Richard Wright, also of Bury St. Edmunds, did the most important work; he painted scenes from Christ's Passion for the chapel. The designs were prepared for him by a man named Busshe, of Bury St. Edmunds. In 1513 Wright agreed with the Master of St. John's College, Cambridge, to carry out an extensive scheme of glazing in that college.

Between 1527 and 1535 he was employed by Sir Thomas Kytson at Hengrave Hall, where some of the shields which he painted are still to be seen.

At the end of the fifteenth century and the beginning of the sixteenth century there is some evidence of the activities of the glass-painters in their guilds. The glaziers of York joined with the saddlers and makers of saddle-trees in presenting 'Jesus destroying Hell: twelve good and twelve evil spirits' in the York mystery plays, presented at the feast of Corpus Christi. At Chester the glaziers, painters, embroiderers, and stationers combined to produce the 'Shepherds' Watch' and 'Angels' Hymn'. These trades, having been joined by custom for the production of this play, received a charter of incorporation in 1534. The play was last produced in 1577. At Norwich the glaziers, bell-founders, braziers, painters, pewterers, and plumbers combined to form the guild of St. Luke. At one time the guild was responsible for the production of the Whit Monday pageants, but in 1527 it successfully petitioned the mayor against this sole responsibility on the grounds of expense. Thereafter twelve pageants were produced, each by a craft or group of crafts at its own expense. The 'Glaziers, Steyners, Screuners, Parchemyners, Carpenters, Gravours, Caryers, Colermakers, Whelewrites' combined to produce 'Helle Carte'.

The glass-painters from the Low Countries mostly settled in Southwark, where English glass-painters had lived and worked as early as 1292. Their presence was bitterly resented and opposed by the London glass-painters. The London guild conducted a vigorous and sustained campaign against them, but the king and at least some of the nobility continued to support the foreigners, and by about the middle of the century the struggle was to all intents and purposes over. There is little to show that foreign glass-painters settled elsewhere in England. If the surname 'Glaswrite' indicates the actual practice of the craft, there seems to have been a group of them at Ipswich just before and during the reign of King Henry VIII. A glazier named John Almayn was working at York in the middle of the century.

The destruction of English medieval glass for about a century after the Reformation was, in general, a gradual process. The monastic churches, except when they were retained to serve as parish churches, must have suffered first and undoubtedly suffered most. It was no longer necessary that their windows should be glazed and many must soon have been emptied for the sake of the lead. The cathedrals, parish churches, college and other chapels presented a problem. An old jest became a real question:

> Demaunde, 'Whiche ben the moost profytable payntes in the chyrche?'
>
> Response, 'They that stonde in the glasse windowes, for they kepe out the wynde for wastynge of the lyghte.'

So William Harrison, looking back over the years, wrote in his *Description of England* in 1577,

> Churches themselves, belles and times of morning & evening praier remain as in time past, saving that all images, shrines, tabernacles, rood loftes & monuments of idolatrie are removed, taken down & defaced: Onlie the stories in glasse windowes excepted, which, for want of sufficient store of new stuffe, & by reason of extreame charge that should grow by the alteration of the same into white panes throughoute the realme, are not altogether abolished in most places at once, but by little and little suffered to decaie that white glass may be set up in their roomes.

The first (1536) and second (1538) Injunctions of King Henry VIII and the Royal Articles of King Edward VI (1547) do not mention stained glass, but part of Article 28 of the Injunctions of 1547 reads:

> *Also*, that they shall take away, utterly extinct and destroy all shrines, coverings of shrines, all tables, candlesticks, trindles or rolls of wax, pictures, paintings, and all other monuments of feigned miracles, pilgrimages, idolatry, and superstition; so that there remain no memory of the same in walls, glass-windows, or elsewhere within their churches or houses. And they shall exhort all their parishioners to do the like within their several houses.

The reports of the churchwardens of a number of the Norwich churches show how fully they acted upon these instructions. Those at St. George, Colegate, wrote, 'Also payde for glasynge of xxviij[ti] wyndows wyth whyght glasse, wyche war glasyd with faynde storys . . . xiiij*li.*'

At St. John, Ber Street, nineteen shillings had been paid 'for makinge of a glasse wyndow wherein Thomas Beckett was'.

At St. Michael-at-Plea they proposed to spend twenty pounds on 'the new glassing of xvij wyndows wherein were conteyned the lyves of certen prophane histories, and other olde wyndows in our church'.

Occasionally the glass was preserved for possible reinstatement or for patching. Thus in 1549 the old glass was taken away from St. Lawrence's church, Reading, and white glass substituted at a cost of £15. 10*s.* 6*d.* There is a note at the end of the churchwardens' accounts for that year, 'It. to remember what was done wth all the old glasse of the wyndows in the churche.'

The authorities became aware of the danger to the fabrics and furniture of the churches if the windows were unglazed. It would also have been impossible to use the churches in the winter unless the windows were boarded up. Article 23 of the Royal Injunctions of 1559 is almost exactly the same as Article 28 of the Injunctions of 1547; but after the words 'within their churches or houses' is added 'preserving nevertheless or repairing the walls and glass windows'. This was re-emphasized in a royal proclamation 'against breaking or defacing of Monuments of Antiquitie, being set up in Churches, or other publike places, for memory, and not for superstition'. It was strictly forbidden to 'breake downe or deface any image in glasse-windowes in any Church, without consent of the Ordinary' upon pain of imprisonment. For many years thereafter the process of decay and replacement with white glass went on, with spasmodic and isolated outbreaks of iconoclasm here and there.

Glass-painting by no means ceased after the Reformation. The painting of sacred imagery must have stopped, but that men should have obeyed the laws of the land and subscribe to the authorized religion of their time did not necessarily mean that they lost their liking for heraldic and other stained glass in the windows of their houses. To read the writings of such antiquaries as Francis Blomefield, Gervase Holles, and Richard Symonds is to be amazed at the vast amount of heraldic glass that was to be seen in the churches and houses which they visited. What is still to be seen is the merest remnant, but a great deal of it, especially in the houses, belongs to the second half of the sixteenth century and to the seventeenth century. Moreover, when Bishop Hooper, in his Injunctions for Gloucester and Worcester, 1551–2, said that if anything in the windows was to be painted, it must not be 'the image or picture of any saint', but 'either branches, flowers or posies taken out of Holy Scripture', he was presumably voicing the feelings of sensible men. It was a religious picture or figure, not stained glass, that was spiritually corrupting and also illegal.

For the years 1550–1600 there are at least thirty shields of arms and other devices which are dated (Pls. 47, 48). The date which accompanies a shield of arms is not always the date of its painting, but there is no reason to think that any of those dates are not contemporary. There is a great deal more which can be dated only approximately, but which must belong to this period (Pl. 46). Much the most distinguished example of glass-painting of this period is the heraldic glass which Bernard Dininckhoff painted for Gilling Castle (Yorks.) in 1585 and later. Dininckhoff's origin is obscure. He may have left south Germany because of the religious troubles of the time. If his history has been made out aright, he was a young man when he produced these windows. He later practised as an architect as well as a glass-painter.

Five years before Dininckhoff signed and dated one of his windows at Gilling Castle, four students of Lincoln's Inn drew up a semi-serious agreement that when any of them should die the survivors should place his armorial bearings in the church where he was buried and also, it would seem, in the churches of the parishes where they themselves were living at the time. The parchment upon which this agreement was recorded is accompanied by another painted with the armorial bearings of those concerned. There is no evidence that the agreement was remembered in later years, but it is interesting in that it shows that at this date a stained-glass window was considered to be a quite natural and usual memorial.

V

THE SEVENTEENTH CENTURY

WELL over one hundred examples of seventeenth-century stained and painted glass are dated. There is a great deal more which can be safely ascribed to this period but cannot be given a definite date.

There were some important changes and developments. One development was of a technical nature. In about the middle of the sixteenth century it was discovered that white glass could be painted with vitreous enamel pigments which were fired in a muffle kiln like the ordinary black pigment which for centuries had been used for painting glass stained wholly or, in the case of ruby glass, partly through its entire substance. Red enamel had been used in this way already. Blue, green, and purple were now introduced. The new technique seems to have been used first in Switzerland. In the beginning this process was used to supplement the older methods of glass-painting, as may be seen in some of the windows of King's College chapel. It was especially useful in the case of heraldic glass and of small panels where the leading-in of small details made the panel clumsy and, when it became dirty, the details indistinct. In this connexion it must also be remembered that heraldic charges were becoming more and more elaborate. Dininckhoff's heraldic glass is a good example of the use of enamel painting to supplement the traditional methods of glass-painting. In a number of places there are quarries beautifully painted with heraldry in enamels and yellow stain.

It cannot be said what course the development of the craft would have taken if it had gone on normally. There was a sudden interruption. The manufacture of coloured glass was centred almost entirely in Lorraine. In 1633 King Louis XIII invaded Lorraine and was strongly resisted by Duke Charles IV. After his victory Louis XIII issued, in 1636, an order 'for razing to the ground and demolishing the palaces and castles of Lorraine'. The glass-painters and their glass-works also disappeared, with the result that in a short space of time 'pot-metal' glass was almost unobtainable. For the time being enamel-painted glass was produced because ordinary stained and painted glass could no longer be provided. There was to be, in course of time, another result of the use of enamels. White glass could be cut into neat rectangular panels and painted. The leads thereby ceased to have their proper significance in emphasizing the design and became only a necessary but tiresome grille or 'fret' covering a painted picture. However, the period of this complete negation of the art did not last long.

In the first part of the seventeenth century there was an important revival of pictorial glass-painting. It was largely due to Archbishop Laud, but others, such as Archbishop Abbot and Bishop Cosin, also encouraged it. The revival is most easily studied in Oxford, where many windows of this date are to be seen. One of the earliest examples is the series of windows in the north and south walls of Wadham College chapel. There are figures of Christ, of prophets, of Apostles, and of St. Stephen. The figure of St. Stephen is dated 1616. The prophets are perhaps a little earlier. The glass may have been painted by Robert Rudland of Oxford. The most striking windows are those painted by Bernard and Abraham van Linge. They were members of a family of glass-painters in Emden. Bernard worked in Paris for four years before coming to England. They left England when the Civil War broke out. Bernard's chief works in Oxford are the east window of Wadham College chapel, with scenes from Christ's Passion, signed and dated 1622; figures of prophets and Apostles in the side windows of Lincoln College chapel, dated 1629 and 1630; a figure of Bishop Oliver King with the ruins of Oseney Abbey in the background in Christ Church, *c.* 1630–40. The scenes in the east window of Wadham College chapel are said to be derived from a plate in Marten de Vos's *Meditationes in Evangelia*, which was printed in Antwerp in 1595. Some of the prophets in the Lincoln College windows are identical in design with those which Bernard painted for the chapel of Lincoln's Inn, London, and the Oseney Abbey background is there used as the background of St. Matthias. The Lincoln's Inn glass was painted in 1623–6. Abraham van Linge painted the scene of 'Jonah before Nineveh' at Christ Church (Pl. 50). It bears the inscription *Abraham van Linge fecit 163..* Most of the other glass which he painted for the cathedral has now gone. In 1635 he painted a great deal of glass for The Queen's College. It has lost much of its significance through being repaired and reset by Joshua Price in 1715–17. In the chapel of Balliol College his representation of the 'Sickness and Recovery of King Hezekiah' is signed and dated 1637. His most successful windows are in the chapel of University College. They are signed and dated 1641. The 'Temptation of Adam and Eve', 'Jacob's Vision', 'Elijah Translated', and 'Jonah and the Whale' are notable achievements.

There is glass of a very different kind in eight windows of the ante-chapel at Magdalen College. It shows figures of female saints and the painting is done in monochrome of a sepia tint. It is the work of Richard Greenbury, goldsmith, glass-painter, portrait-painter, and copyist of pictures. He supplied glass to the college in 1632. Greenbury was probably also responsible for the beautiful portraits on glass which are to be seen in a number of the Oxford colleges. Two of the best are the portraits of King Charles I and his Queen in the hall of Magdalen College (Pl. 51). One is dated 1633. They are copied from prints by W. J. Duff, engraved in 1628 and 1630, after oil paintings by Daniel Mytens.

The glass in the east window of the chapel of Trinity Hospital, Greenwich, was probably painted in 1616. It shows the 'Crucifixion' flanked by the 'Agony in the Garden' and the 'Ascension'. The lower part of the window contains heraldic glass of the same date. The artist is unknown. Two windows in the chapel of the Holy Trinity at Guildford contain glass painted by an English glass-painter, Baptista Sutton, and dated 1621. They show heraldry in the upper parts and the story of Jacob and Esau in the lower parts. In 1634 Sutton painted the glass which was in the east window of St. Leonard's, Shoreditch, until it was mostly destroyed by a bomb in the last war. The beautiful east window of the chapel of Peterhouse, Cambridge, was painted in 1632. It has been suggested that it, too, is Sutton's work, but the ascription is inadmissible on stylistic grounds. It may be recalled that Bishop Cosin's glass in the Peterhouse chapel windows and another window by Sutton in a church at Tothilfields figured in the trial of Archbishop Laud. Rather in the style of the van Linges and about contemporary with their work is an interesting window showing the 'Baptism of Christ' in Compton church (Surrey). Very different is the glass put by Lord Scudamore into the Herefordshire churches of Sellack (*c.* 1630–50) and Abbey Dore (1634).

The date 1638 is noteworthy because in that year the London glaziers' guild became a City Company under a charter granted by King Charles I.

The period of the Commonwealth brought the revival of pictorial stained glass to an end. There was a much greater outburst of zealous iconoclasm than there had been hitherto. The writings of the seventeenth-century and eighteenth-century antiquaries show that the soldiery and others of the Commonwealth period have been blamed for many losses which were, in fact, caused by ignorance and neglect in later years. Nevertheless, there is no doubt that great damage was done at this time. In 1640 a new campaign against 'superstitious pictures', images, ornaments, and relics of 'idolatry' was launched and was authorized by the House of Commons in 1643. There were dramatic and dreadful happenings. William Dowsing, appointed a Parliamentary Visitor in December 1643, kept a diary of his progress of destruction in Suffolk. It shows how much had survived in the churches up to that time. He also ravaged the town and county of Cambridge. In 1644 committees were formed in Norwich 'to view the churches for pictures and crucifixes', and the churches were ruthlessly stripped. In the same year some of the townsfolk wrought havoc in the cathedral and in the chapel of the bishop's palace, driving Bishop Hall from his home. A petition, said to have been signed by twelve thousand 'Weamen of Middlesex', says, 'We desire that prophane glass windowes, whose superstitious paint makes many idolaters, may be humbled and dashed in pieces against the ground; for our conscions tell us that they are diabolicall, and the father of Darkness was the inventor of them, being the chief Patron of damnable pride'. The cathedrals of Chester, Lichfield, Peterborough, and Winchester were damaged, to a greater or less extent, by various Parliamentary armies. At Christ Church, Oxford, one of the canons 'furiously stamped upon the windows of his cathedral when taken down, utterly defacing them'. At Canterbury Richard Culmer, rector of Chartham, did his best to destroy as much glass as he could. When he got to the 'Royal' window he stood 'on the top of the citie ladder, near 60 steps high, with a whole pike in his hand ratling down proud Becket's glassy bones'. He then published, in 1644, an account of his activities entitled *Cathedrall Newes from Canterbury*. Most records of what happened are not so picturesque. They conform more to the laconic entry in the churchwardens' accounts for 1643 at Toft Monks in Norfolk: 'Laid out to Ruseles the glaysher for taken Down of the painted Glase, 1*s*. 6*d*.'

Bishop Hall, in his *Hard Measure*, tells how, having stood and argued with the iconoclasts in his chapel, he removed only the heads of the saints in the windows. At about the same time the vicar of Owthorpe (Notts.) removed the heads from the stained-glass windows in his church 'and laid them carefully up in his closet'. Colonel Hutchinson, Governor of Nottingham, went to Owthorpe and persuaded him to destroy the stained glass and the wall-paintings, 'which he consented to do, but being ill-affected, was one of those who began to brand Mr. Hutchinson with the name of puritan'. In many places the crucifixes and the heads of the saints were removed or destroyed and the rest of the glass was allowed to remain. For instance, in New College chapel, Oxford, at Gipping (Suff.), Marsh Baldon, and elsewhere the representation of Christ on the cross is completely or almost completely destroyed, but the figures of the Blessed Virgin Mary and St. John Evangelist have survived. At such places as Great Massingham (Norf.), where all the heads of the Apostles have gone, and Shotwick (Ches.), where a similar fate has befallen the two beautiful figures in a fourteenth-century representation of the 'Annunciation', the heads must have been purposely removed or broken. In York Minster it may be observed that, in panel after panel, the original heads have disappeared. At Barton Mills (Suff.) someone destroyed not only the heads of the saints in the main lights, but also the heads of all the dragons which occupy the tracery lights. Similarly, on many East Anglian rood screens the faces of the saints have been scratched across, but their figures are left untouched.

Examples of pictorial windows on a large scale painted during the second half of the seventeenth century are uncommon. The best are those painted by Henry Gyles of York (1645–1709). There is a fine, though somewhat restored, example, painted in 1676 and signed, in Staveley church (Derby.) (Pl. 55) and another, painted in 1681, in Adel church (Yorks.). To the next century belong the glass in the Fairfax chapel, Denton-in-Wharfedale (Yorks.) (1702) and another window in Adel church (1706). There is the much-restored glass in the three great lancets at the west end of Wells Cathedral. As much of it as is original was painted between 1660 and 1672. There is also the remarkable east window of Low Ham church (Som.) which was probably painted about 1690 (Pl. 55). In 1696 William Price painted a window showing the 'Nativity of Christ' for Christ Church, Oxford. Parts of it are preserved in a clerestory window in the north transept.

Throughout the century much heraldic glass was produced. Many examples are dated and some are of great merit. Good examples of various dates are the royal arms, *temp.* Charles I, at Barningham Winter (Norf.) (Pl. 52), the early seventeenth-century achievement of Hall in South Newington church (Oxon.) (Pl. 48), and the mid-seventeenth-century armorial glass at Stoke Poges (Bucks.) (Pl. 53). A very ornate heraldic window, dated 1687, by an unknown artist, at St. Andrew's, Holborn, was destroyed in the last war. In a window of Holy Trinity church, Shaftesbury (Dorset) there is a shield of arms with the following inscription beneath it:

GOOD MEN NEED NOT MARBLE
WEE DARE TRVST TO GLASS THE
MEMORY OF WILLIAM WHITAKER ESQ.
WHO DIED THE 3RD OF OCTOBER 1616

There is other seventeenth-century glass besides the large pictorial window and heraldry. For instance, in about 1600 an unknown and probably local glass-painter produced an interesting series of roundels, with texts from the Bible, Latin authors, and other sources, for the windows of Preston Hall, Suffolk. The texts are written upon elaborately coiled ribbons. Some of these roundels are now in the Victoria and Albert Museum (Pl. 49). To about the year 1621 belong the series of quarries, painted with morris dancers, once in Betley Hall (Staffs.) and now in private possession. In Tolson Hall, Strickland Ketel (Westmorland) there are quarries dated 1638. One shows three pipes, two plugs of tobacco, and the inscription, *God by this means hath sent, what I on this house have spent. T.T. 1638.* Another has three plugs of tobacco and the additional inscription, *All prayers be unto His name, that gave me means to build the same.* A third shows a female figure, probably representing 'Faith'. In the windows of Hale Hall (Lancs.) there was much early seventeenth-century glass which has now passed into a private collection. There are representations of the 'Twelve Months' (of which four are lost), the 'Four Seasons', and twelve equestrian figures of the Caesars. The figures all have accompanying verses, some of which are far from successful. Thus Domitian has:

This Caeſar to his Countrey was a blott
And blemiſh by his vices w[ch] he gott
He in his life much imitates the Apes
And Proteus like tranſformes into all ſhapes
But when his Gods for to contemne he ſought
He by his ffreindes unto his death was brought.

A favourite device during this period was the stained-glass sundial. A large number remain, although not all are in a perfect state of preservation. There are many designs. Common to most of them is the painting of a fly, which is given an extraordinary reality by painting its body on one side of the glass and its head on the other. Sometimes the middle of the dial has a bird looking at a fly. In some examples there is an hour-glass flanked by wings at the top of the panel. All this is a play upon the motto often painted on the dial, *Dum spectas fugio.* At Winchester College there is a dial in the middle of which is a post around which is a scroll inscribed *Vt umbra ſit vita tranſit.* The dial at Bucklebury church (Berks.) is dated 1649 and inscribed *S.S. me fecit* (Pl. 54). There is another like it, but dated 1641, at Warnefield Place (Wilts.). In these examples, as in another, dated 1664, at Park Hall, Leigh (Staffs.), a shield of arms is painted in the middle of the dial. The fine example at Nun Appleton Hall (Yorks.) was painted in 1670 by Henry Gyles, the York glass-painter. The middle of the dial is occupied by the representation of a cupid after an engraving after Titian, and the four corners of the panel have representations of the 'Four Seasons'. For a sundial, complete with brass gnomon, Gyles charged a pound. When a whole window was commissioned, he sometimes gave a sundial with it.

VI

THE EIGHTEENTH CENTURY

CERTAIN names are prominent in the history of eighteenth-century glass-painting. They are the Price family; William Peckitt of York, 1731–95; Francis Eginton of Birmingham, 1737–1805; James Pearson, born 1750, and Eglington Margaret his wife; Thomas Jervais, died 1799.

William Price the elder is thought to have learnt his art from Edmund Gyles of York. The glass which he painted in 1711–12 for the east window of Merton College chapel, Oxford, has been taken out and stored. His 'Nativity of Christ' window in Christ Church, Oxford, has already been mentioned. Joshua Price, William's younger brother, is well represented by glass in The Queen's College, Oxford, and ten windows in Great Witley church (Worcs.) (Pl. 59). He also painted glass, after designs by Sir James Thornhill, for the rose window in the north transept of Westminster Abbey. William Price, son of William Price the elder, painted the fine series of five windows on the south side of the chapel of New College, Oxford. He incorporated some of the original fourteenth-century glass, especially in his canopies. He made the windows between 1735 and 1740 and was paid £84 for each of them. In 1735 he was also painting the glass for the west window of Westminster Abbey.

William Peckitt's work was extensive. Until it was destroyed in the last war there was in the Old Council Chamber at York glass which he painted in 1735 when he was twenty-two years of age and for which he was granted the freedom of the city free of charge. It showed the arms of the city in the upper part and 'Justice riding in a Triumphal Car' in the lower part. Among his many other works are the windows on the south side of the chapel of New College. The figures, except two later ones by William Raphael Eginton, in the two easternmost windows were painted in 1765 for the great west window of the chapel, but were moved to their present position when it was decided to put the Jervais-Reynolds window there. The other windows, based upon designs by Biagio Rebecca and showing figures of Adam, Eve, patriarchs, and prophets, were painted in 1772–4. They are startling productions with a bold range of colours and an individual interpretation of the Gothic style which was not well-pleasing to the College. Good examples of his pictorial windows are his 'Presentation of Christ in the Temple' (1767), after a design by Dr. Wall, in Oriel College, Oxford, and his 'Last Supper' (1770) in Rothwell church (Yorks.). Even more notable is a window in the library of Trinity College, Cambridge. It shows Alma Mater (the Spirit of Cambridge) presenting Isaac Newton to King George III. Francis Bacon, in the Chancellor's robes, records the introduction. Fame flies through the clouds announcing the news. Minerva stands behind the throne (Pl. 61). This window was designed by Giovanni Battista Cipriani and completed by Peckitt in 1775. Peckitt also painted the 'Last Supper' for the east window of the chapel of Audley End in 1771 (Pl. 62). This window, like three of the New College windows, was designed by Biagio Rebecca, whose designs in both cases have been preserved. Peckitt's heraldic glass may be seen in the churches of Coxwold and Harpham (Yorks.). He restored many windows in York Minster and worked for Horace Walpole at Strawberry Hill.

Francis Eginton was one of a number of men whom Matthew Boulton employed in his factory, the Soho, in Birmingham. He superintended the japanned ware department. He also made models to be cast in metal. Later he associated with Boulton in reproductions, called 'polygraphs', of well-known pictures. Eginton became a popular glass-painter. When Nelson and Lady Hamilton visited him in his home, Prospect Hill, at Handsworth, flowers were strewn on the path up to his house and the bells of Handsworth church were rung. One of his best-known windows, showing the 'Conversion of St. Paul', is in St. Paul's church, Birmingham. It is based upon a picture by Sir Benjamin West, Eginton paying eighty guineas for the loan of it. He painted the

'Resurrection of Christ', after Reynolds, for the cathedrals of Lichfield and Salisbury, and the 'Resurrection of Lady Letitia Dearden' for Aston church, Birmingham, as well as many other windows for churches and houses, including Fonthill Abbey.

James Pearson, who was born in Dublin, settled in London. He painted windows for a number of London churches, for Salisbury Cathedral, and for Brasenose College, Oxford. Eglington Margaret Pearson also painted windows, such as one after Guido's 'Aurora' for Arundel Castle.

Thomas Jervais was, like James Pearson, born in Dublin. He and his brother worked there for a while before seeking greater opportunities in London. He later moved to Windsor. He painted the 'Nativity' and the 'Virtues' for the great west window of New College chapel (Pl. 63). They are based upon designs painted by Sir Joshua Reynolds. The window was completed in 1783. Opinions vary, and have always varied, about it. James Woodforde the diarist said of the 'Virtues', 'No Painting can exceed them I think on glass', and Fanny Burney wrote of 'the beautiful window of Sir Joshua Reynolds and Mr. Jervis'. Horace Walpole speaks of 'Sir Joshua's washy Virtues', and Lord Torrington saw them as 'half-dressed languishing Harlots'. The window is a landmark, if also a low-water mark, in the history of English glass-painting. Soon after he had finished the New College window Jervais, with his pupil Forrest, painted a very large representation of the 'Resurrection' for the east window of St. George's chapel, Windsor. It has since been removed. It was designed by Benjamin West, whom Jervais had recommended as the designer of the New College window. They combined to produce other windows.

These were the chief men. There were others less well known. For instance, there was John Rowell, 'at Wycomb in Buckinghamshire', who advertised himself in *The Craftsman* in 1733 as reviving and performing 'the antient art of staining glass' and as maker of sundials and coats of arms for windows. It was probably his son who, eleven years later, advertised himself in *The Reading Mercury* as 'the performer of several large pieces of History &c in stained glass'. He also lived at High Wycombe. John Rowell the elder produced the heraldic glass in Harpsden church (Oxon.) in 1733. In 1770 John Rowell the younger painted a window showing the 'Adoration of the Shepherds' for the chapel of The Vyne (Pl. 60). There was also John Langton, who flourished in the years 1700–27 and kept a school at Stamford (Lincs.). He published a copy-book with his 'effigies' on the title-page and, below it, the statement that he 'in the year 1700 Revived the Noble Art of Glass-Painting, Staining and Tinging in the way of the Antients'. In the preface he offers, among other things, to paint for 'such gentlemen as are curious . . . the Squares of their Sash-Windows . . . with flowers'.

There must have been a number of other local glass-painters whose names are at present unknown. Such men produced the charming little panel, dated 1701, in Hertford Museum (Pl. 57) and the shields of arms at Bradenham (Bucks.) and Turville (Bucks.) (Pl. 57).

Some of the glass-painters, like Gyles and Peckitt, made great efforts to obtain 'pot-metal' glass for their windows. Gyles, in a letter written at the end of the seventeenth century, says that he is enclosing 'some specimens of my owne coloured glasse' and goes on to say that they are pieces of glass left over from the window which he painted for University College, Oxford. He says further that he could make large quantities of it if he were encouraged to do so. Coloured glass was certainly being made in England half a century later. For instance, Dr. Richard Pococke says in his *Travels through England*: '1751 8 June, came to Stourbridge, famous for its glass-manufacture which is here coloured in the liquid in all the capital colours in their several shades, and if I mistake not, is a secret which they have here.' The really important glass, 'flashed' ruby (that is to say, clear glass coated with a thin layer of red glass), was apparently unobtainable. Glass as nearly red as possible was produced by staining the glass several times by the old 'yellow stain' process. Peckitt, however, experimented in making coloured glass and seems to have produced glass 'flashed' with several colours. The method of making 'flashed' ruby is generally said to have been rediscovered by Bontemps in 1826, but in the church of

St. Michael, Spurriergate, York, there is a piece of flashed ruby engraved (by grinding away the 'flashed' colour on a wheel) *J. Barnett 1821.*

It should be remembered that in this century there were men who were interested to collect English medieval glass. Horace Walpole, Lord Torrington, and William Cole of Milton were acquiring what they could even if James Wyatt the architect was causing the 'grisaille' glass to be cleared out of the windows of Salisbury Cathedral and thrown into the 'Town Ditch'.

VII

THE NINETEENTH CENTURY

IT is customary to call all nineteenth-century stained glass 'Victorian' and to dismiss it as unworthy of serious consideration. As Queen Victoria was born in 1819 and died in 1901, the term 'Victorian' is a reasonable description of it. To imply that all the stained-glass windows produced in the nineteenth century are so bad that they must be ignored is ridiculous. There are some windows which are very good and others which are very bad. A great number are merely dull. The revival of interest in Gothic architecture, the building of many new churches, the partial or total rebuilding of many ancient churches in the Gothic style, had a profound effect upon glass-painting. Stained-glass windows were everywhere demanded and strenuous efforts were made to go back to the designs if not always to the subject-matter of the medieval windows.

At the beginning of the century several men stand out as painters of interesting windows. William Raphael Eginton (1778–1834) was the son of Francis Eginton. He executed works for King George IV and was appointed glass-painter to Princess Charlotte. He produced many windows, especially for the mansions of the nobility. For instance, in conjunction with his brother-in-law Samuel Lowe, he filled the great library window at Stourhead (Wilts.), with a copy of Raphael's 'School of Athens'. Other good examples of his work may be seen in Barr chapel, near Chester, and in the churches of Brockley (Som.) (Pl. 66), Colley (Yorks.), Digswell (Herts.), and Hatton (Warwick.). There is also the firm of Betton and Evans of Shrewsbury. Sir John Betton, son of John Betton, glazier, was admitted to the Glaziers' Company in 1775 and died in 1849. David Evans was admitted to the Glaziers' Company in 1819. His son Charles later joined the firm, which produced many windows from 1820 onwards. They are mostly to be seen in Shropshire churches, and chiefly in Shrewsbury. Charles Evans later moved to London. In the years 1822–8 the firm produced the excellent copies of the fourteenth-century glass in the chapel of Winchester College (Pl. 65). In 1838 they painted the two windows still to be seen at the west end of the chapel of Wadham College, Oxford. An example of their armorial glass is a window (1833) at Kenilworth (Warwick.). Another glass-painter of the time was Joseph Backler, who 'by his talent and genius extended the powers of the art of glass-painting almost beyond hope of its eventual perfection'. Among his works is a representation of the 'Resurrection' (1821), with the figure of Christ taken from Raphael's 'Transfiguration' in St. Thomas's church, Dudley (Pl. 64), and the heraldic glass (1857) at Sutton Place, Guildford. In 1817 he exhibited at the Stained Glass Works, 18 Newman Street, London, windows including 'King John signing Magna Carta', after James Lonsdale, which he made for Arundel Castle, and 'Eruption of Mount Vesuvius', after Pether. Another glass-painter worthy of notice is Bradley, who designed the east window for Francis Johnson's Chapel Royal in the Castle of Dublin. Unknown artists of this period produced interesting windows which survive in the churches of Raithby-by-Louth and Radbourne (Lincs.).

An outstanding figure is Thomas Willement (1786–1871), 'Heraldic Artist to King George IV', and 'Artist in Stained Glass to Queen Victoria'. He did more than anyone else to restore heraldic stained glass to its proper place of dignity and importance. A privately printed book, dated 1840, records all his work from 1812 to that year. It shows how much he produced and how widely his windows were dispersed even during those early years. For instance, in 1835 he painted windows for fourteen different places and in 1838 for twenty-seven different places. Perhaps his best work is the big memorial window in the great hall at Hampton Court.

From the twenty-four firms which showed stained glass in the Great Exhibition of 1851, O'Connor of London, Hedgeland of London, W. Wailes of Newcastle-upon-Tyne, and Gibbs of London may be picked out. O'Connor's work is well shown in the windows of the chancel of Bardwell church (Suff.) (Pl. 69). Hedgeland is best known for his restorations of the ancient glass in the chapel of King's College, Cambridge, and the church of St. Neot (Corn.). One of the most remarkable of his own windows is the west window of Norwich Cathedral. M. R. James suggested that eyes should as much as possible be averted from it as being 'the gravest of insults to the memory of the excellent Bishop Stanley'. It has, in fact, much to commend it. The work of the Wailes family is well represented in the church of St. John Baptist, Newcastle. The mosaic-like work of Gibbs is best seen in the south aisle windows (1849) of All Saints, Margaret Street, London.

There are very few churches which do not contain at least one stained-glass window produced in the second half of the nineteenth century. Like the art of any period this glass reflects to a considerable extent contemporary thought and values. As such it is a much more significant social document than is generally realized. The subject-matter and the manner of its representation do much to interpret and preserve the outlook of the times. For instance, the text 'Suffer little children to come unto me' is illustrated with great frequency in Victorian stained glass. The figure of Christ may now appear as unworthy as the figures of the children are unreal, but the glass-painter produced them and the donor accepted them as adequate exemplars of the scene and thereby revealed their own state of mind.

There is a window at Wimpole (Cambs.) in memory of Victor Alexander Yorke, third son of the fourth Earl of Hardwick (Pl. 68). He died suddenly on 23 December 1867, while reciting

> Willy, my beauty, my eldest-born, the flower of the flock;
> Never a man could fling him, for Willy stood like a rock.

from Tennyson's *The Grandmother*, at a village gathering. The window shows him, in the uniform of a Lieutenant of the Royal Horse Artillery, conducting a Penny Reading or, perhaps, a Bible Class. The words 'Adonai, Adonai, Thy children come' are written in the window. They are the words of a song which he had sung 'most beautifully and dramatically' earlier in the evening. The window, which is very well painted, conveys the period as well as a panel of the 'St. William' window at York conveys the fifteenth century. Similarly, the time of Queen Victoria's 1887 Jubilee is excellently preserved in a window commemorating it in Great Malvern priory church (Pl. 71). It was painted by Messrs. Winfield Ltd. (later Messrs. Camm & Co.) of Birmingham. They managed to produce a wealth of detail, especially in the three panels at the bottom of the window, without loss of luminosity.

In order to appreciate the full colour, vigour, and life of Victorian glass at its best it is necessary to find a church, preferably built at about the same time that the glass was painted, where all, or nearly all, the windows are filled with glass produced during that period. St. Mary's, Stratfield Mortimer (Berks.) is such a church. There is a window, hidden by the organ, containing earlier and interesting glass, English and foreign, and there is a chapel with two windows filled with good twentieth-century glass by Messrs. James Powell and Sons (Whitefriars), Ltd., but the other windows show what an effect Victorian glass, painted by O'Connor and others, can produce. Ely Cathedral is an example of a great medieval building in which almost every window is filled with glass painted in the second half of the nineteenth century. Much of the glass is in the style of the thirteenth century, but in some windows, as in a notable representation of the 'Elijah Translated' in the north aisle of the nave, the artist has had a freer hand.

It should be remembered that churches are not the only buildings in which Victorian stained glass is preserved. The rest of the ground is well covered in some remarks on 'Glass Staining' which a famous firm of glass-painters included in its *Illustrated Catalogue of Stained Glass Windows*.

> Public buildings offer most appropriate opportunities for stained glass decoration—historical events, public characters, and armorial bearings, furnishing unlimited subjects for illustration in harmony with the character and purposes of the erection; and it is gratifying to see the extent to which this art is adopted in the decoration of our national and municipal buildings, and other places of public assembly.

The varied resources of Glass Staining are equally suitable for the decoration of mansions, affording an exquisite adornment for the windows of halls, corridors, staircases, &c., and in many cases effectually screening the objectionable sights at the back of the house. For these purposes, simple and beautiful patterns of rich colours may be produced at very moderate expense. Family events and ancestral achievements afford subjects for windows of a higher character, approximating in effect to the magnificence of those in ecclesiastical edifices. Intermediate between the two, *Heraldry* holds its place as the most general and beautiful decoration for mansions.

The work of several men and firms must be mentioned as representative of the best windows of the period. The windows of Charles Eamer Kempe (1837–1907) vary in quality, but always repay examination. An early (1874) example, once in his own house, Old Place, Lindfield, and now in Wightwick Manor, Wolverhampton, illustrates 'Summer' ('And through another saw the summer glow') from William Morris's *Earthly Paradise* (Pl. 70). A particularly good example of his work is the 'Milton' window in Horton church (Bucks.). The firm of Clayton and Bell is well known. John Richard Clayton (1827–1913) and Alfred Bell (1832–95), during forty years of unbroken harmony, co-operated to produce a great many windows. It is impossible to find one of their windows that is shoddy or ugly, but some of them are dull. They followed, perhaps too strictly, medieval precedents of design, but at times, as in the great series of windows in the cathedrals at Bury St. Edmunds and Truro, they achieved real richness and beauty. It is interesting to see the development of the Bell family's style through the second, third, and fourth generation. Nathaniel Hubert John Westlake (1833–1921) is well known to students of ancient stained glass for his valuable *History of Design in Painted Glass* (1894). Typical examples of his windows are in Worcester Cathedral and the churches of St. John Baptist, Brighton, St. John the Divine, Richmond, the Sacred Heart, Hove, and St. Philip Neris, Arundel. Henry Holiday (1839–1927) produced windows for churches, chapels, and other buildings all over the world. The windows in the chapel of Worcester College, Oxford, are fair examples of his early (1864–5) work. Some are more successful in design and colouring than others; the 'Ascension' is the best. He also decorated the walls and the ceiling of the chapel in 1864–5. One of his single figures is well shown in St. John's church, Stratfield Mortimer (Berks.).

A firm whose work in the nineteenth and twentieth centuries cannot be ignored is John Hardman & Co. (later John Hardman's Studios) of Birmingham. Its earliest windows are among the most interesting of the 'Gothic revival' experiments. The later windows are nearly always good. There is, for instance, the interesting 'Te Deum' window, which the firm executed after a design by A. W. Pugin, in the south transept of Sherborne Abbey. The 'Transfiguration' in the east window of Bury St. Edmunds Cathedral is one of the finest works produced by any nineteenth-century glass-painter (Pl. 67).

The influence and significance of Edward Burne-Jones (1833–98) and William Morris (1834–96) were as great in stained glass as in other forms of art. Burne-Jones drew his first cartoons for stained glass in 1857. His 'St. Frideswide' window in Christ Church, Oxford, was produced in 1859. Another example of his early work is in Bradfield College. At this time he designed windows for Messrs. James Powell & Sons. He ceased to work for them in 1861, when Henry Holiday took his place, and he thereafter worked only for his friend William Morris. Morris held fast to two principles. First, he separated the work of the artist and the craftsman, on the principle that a good artist is not necessarily a good craftsman and a good craftsman may not be a good artist. He obtained the best artists that he could find to design his windows and then adapted the designs to his medium. In time his designs came almost entirely from Burne-Jones's studio. In many of the 'Burne-Jones' windows, the figure-work is by Burne-Jones and the background and foliage are Morris's work. Second, he refused, with few exceptions, to make stained-glass windows for buildings which, in his opinion, were ancient monuments. There are many examples of their later work, such as the 'St. Cecilia' (1874–5) and 'St. Catherine' (1878) windows in Christ Church, Oxford, and two windows in Salisbury Cathedral (1879). Perhaps the finest are those in Birmingham Cathedral (Pl. 72).

An important thread in the history of nineteenth-century stained glass is the struggle to obtain a less flat and more luminous range of coloured glass with which to work. Charles Winston (1814–65) was a pioneer in this direction. Although the law was his profession, the study of stained glass was his passion. He probably did more than any other man to make known the value and interest of ancient stained glass and to emphasize the need to improve the quality of the stained glass used in making new windows. After collaborating with several small London firms in attempting to produce better glass, he joined with Messrs. James Powell & Sons of Whitefriars, and together they effected a considerable improvement in the glass. Thereafter J. R. Clayton, at the instance of Gilbert Scott, made a careful study of ancient and modern stained glass at home and abroad, with a view to improving the art as a whole. He met William Edward Chance, who had a wide experience of English and foreign methods of making glass. Chance, after years of experiments in his glass-works at Oldbury, produced results, especially in the making of red glass, far superior to anything that had been produced since medieval times. He was first successful in producing 'antique' glass in 1863. The first window in which it was used was by Hardman. Other 'antique' glass was soon to be made by Lloyd and Summerfield of Birmingham, and Hartley's (later Hartley, Wood & Co.) of Sunderland, both of whom were closely connected with Chance in 1870–2, when many obstacles connected with the construction of furnaces and the making of special colours were overcome.

VIII

THE TWENTIETH CENTURY

IT is difficult to choose between the twentieth-century windows, but it is even more difficult to believe that some of them will not eventually stand out as of greater excellence and interest than others. There is, for instance, the work of Christopher Whall (1850–1924), many of whose windows were produced in conjunction with his son and daughter, Christopher and Veronica Whall. Some of his best-known windows are in the Lady chapel in Gloucester Cathedral. There are others of outstanding merit in Ashbourne church (Derby.) (Pl. 73), in Leicester Cathedral, and in Tonbridge School chapel. Anyone who visits the church of the Ascension, Bitterne Park, Southampton, and studies the series of windows by Archibald Keightley Nicholson (1872–1937) and G. E. R. Smith must see that they are a great achievement (Pl. 75), as are many other of their windows such as those at Balsham (Cambs.) and Crewkerne (Som.). It was largely due to Nicholson and to Reginald Bell that the modern glass-painter has come to realize that a window is put into a wall to admit light and that a stained-glass window need not be all stained glass. Nicholson also displayed great ingenuity in combining large figures and small scenes in a single composition. The windows designed by Douglas Strachan (1875–1950) are also unforgettable. The finest examples of his work in England are the windows in the churches of Hotham (Yorks.) and Winchelsea (Sussex) (Pl. 74). He had no rival in the use of colour and the suggestion of movement in the representation of such subjects as the 'Creation' and scenes from the Revelation of St. John the Divine. The windows of Reginald Bell (1886–1950) often 'derive' from the windows of the fifteenth century but always bear the unmistakable stamp of his own individuality. His 'Victory' window (1920) in Salisbury Cathedral has been described by a discerning critic as 'one of the finest painted during the past 400 years'. The series of historic medieval personages and heraldic panels (1930) in St. Mary's Hall, Coventry, are at least as fine as the Salisbury Cathedral window and, by great good fortune, survived the bombing of the city. No modern glass-painter has produced better groups of 'St. George and the Dragon' than those in Exeter Cathedral and Exford church (Som.). Martin Travers's windows are always noteworthy and, like his reredoses, add beauty to any church in which they have been placed. His own favourite window was the 'St. Nicholas' window (1928) in St. Sampson's church, Cricklade (Wilts.). It shows his skill in combining a main subject (St. Nicholas standing in a ship) with an heraldic achievement and a bold inscription. Another window which shows how well he could combine large figures and small groups in a harmonious design is at Ilkley (Yorks.). James H. Hogan (1883–1948), who worked with James Powell and Sons, was a glass-painter who steadily developed a style of his own. This development is well seen in his windows in Liverpool Cathedral. In the Lady chapel are his earliest windows which were designed when he was working with J. W. Brown, a disciple of Burne-Jones. In the choir and south-west transept are the windows upon which he was working when he died. They replaced earlier windows of his which had been destroyed by bombs. He had come to rely almost wholly on plain colour and thick black lines, abandoning half-tones and shading. The differences of his style are observable when comparison is made between such windows as the 'St. Francis' window in the chapel of Christ's Hospital, Hertford, and his window in the Chapel of Ease, Warninglid (Sussex). The windows of F. C. Eden (1864–1944) are sometimes, perhaps, too 'sentimental', but they are cool, calm, and beautifully executed. There are typical examples at Clare (Suff.) and Thorpe (Derby.) (Pl. 76).

These are, perhaps, the chief names, but others are noteworthy. For instance, T. F. Curtis did beautiful work for Messrs. Ward & Hughes. A good example, dated 1908, can be seen in the chapel of Bloxham School. Again, Hugh Arnold designed a most attractive window for Saxlingham Nethergate church in 1910.

It would be unprofitable to attempt to discriminate between the stained glass of contemporary workers in this field or to forecast what future generations will have to say about their windows, but it is certain that the work of Sir Ninian Comper (Pl. 79), Hugh Easton (Pl. 80), Evie Hone (Pl. 79) and Christopher Webb (Pl. 77) will stand out as of major importance.

BIBLIOGRAPHY

An Inventory of the Historical Monuments in the City of Oxford: Royal Commission on Historical Monuments, England. London, 1939.

Anon., 'Reginald Bell, 1886–1950. Artist in Stained Glass', in *Studio*, vol. cxli, no. 698.

BALDRY, A. L., *Henry Holiday*, Walker's Quarterly, nos. 31–32. London, 1930.

CHATWIN, P. B., 'Medieval Stained Glass from the Cathedral, Coventry', in *Transactions of the Birmingham Archaeological Society*, vol. lxvi.

—— 'Some Notes on the Painted Windows of the Beauchamp Chapel, Warwick', in ibid., vol. liii.

CLARK-MAXWELL, W. G., 'An Heraldic Agreement of 1580', in *Antiquaries Journal*, vol. xiii.

COLVIN, H. M., 'Medieval Glass from Dale Abbey', in *Derbyshire Archaeological and Natural History Society's Journal*, 1939.

A description of the glass in Morley church, Derbyshire.

DORLING, E. E., *Leopards of England and other Papers on Heraldry.* London, 1912.

DRAKE, F. M., 'The Fourteenth-century Stained Glass of Exeter Cathedral', in *Transactions of the Devonshire Association for the Advancement of Science, Literature, and Art*, vol. xliv.

EELES, F. C., and PEATLING, A. V., *Ancient Stained and Painted Glass in the Churches of Surrey.* Surrey Archaeological Society, 1930.

FOWLER, J., 'On a Window representing the Life and Miracles of S. William of York, at the North End of the Eastern Transept, York Minster', in *Yorkshire Archaeological Journal*, vol. iii.

FRANKS, A. W., *A Book of Ornamental Glazing Quarries, Collected and Arranged from Ancient Examples.* London, 1849.

GARROD, H. W., *Ancient Painted Glass in Merton College, Oxford.* London, 1931.

GREEN, M. A., 'Old Painted Glass in Worcestershire', in *Transactions of the Worcestershire Archaeological Society*, New Series, vols. xi–xxiv.

HARDY, C. F., 'On the Music in the Painted Glass of the Windows in the Beauchamp Chapel at Warwick', in *Archaeologia*, vol. lxi.

HARRISON, F., *The Painted Glass of York.* London, 1927.

HARRISON, K., *The Windows of King's College, Cambridge: Notes on their History and Design.* Cambridge, 1952.

HUTCHINSON, F. E., *Medieval Glass at All Souls College.* London, 1949.

JAMES, M. R., *A Guide to the Windows of King's College Chapel, Cambridge*, with an appendix by E. Milner-White. Cambridge, 1930.

Journal of the British Society of Master Glass-Painters, 1924–52.
JOYCE, J. G., *The Fairford Windows*. London, 1872.
KNOWLES, J. A., 'Additional Notes on the St. William Window in York Minster', in *Proceedings of the Yorkshire Architectural and York Archaeological Society*, vol. I.
—— 'Disputes between English and Foreign Glass-Painters in the Sixteenth Century', in *Antiquaries Journal*, vol. v.
—— *Essays in the History of the York School of Glass-Painting*. London, 1936.
—— 'Henry Gyles, Glass-Painter of York', in *Walpole Society Publications*, vol. xi.
—— 'On Two Panels of Glass in the Bodleian Library representing Scenes from the History of St. Thomas Becket', in *Bodleian Quarterly Record*, vol. v.
—— 'Stained Glass Sundials', in *Connoisseur*, vol. lxxxv, no. 344.
—— 'Technical Notes on the St. William Window in York Minster', in *Yorkshire Archaeological Journal*, vol. xxxvii.
—— 'The Transition from the Mosaic to the Enamel Method of Painting on Glass', in *Antiquaries Journal*, vol. vi.
—— 'The West Window, St. Martin-le-Grand, Coney Street, York', in *Yorkshire Archaeological Journal*, vol. xxxviii.
—— 'William Peckitt, Glass-Painter', in *Walpole Society Publications*, vol. xvii.
LAFOND, J., 'The Stained Glass Decoration of Lincoln Cathedral in the Thirteenth Century', in *Archaeological Journal*, vol. ciii.
LAMBORN, E. A. GREENING, *The Armorial Glass of the Oxford Diocese, 1250–1850*. London, 1949.
LE COUTEUR, J. D., *Ancient Glass in Winchester*. Winchester, 1920.
LETHABY, W. R., 'Archbishop Roger's Cathedral at York and its Stained Glass', in *Archaeological Journal*, vol. lxxii.
MILNER-WHITE, E., in *The Friends of York Minster Annual Report*, 1946–52.
NELSON, P., 'Ancient Glass from Hale Hall, Lancashire', in *Transactions of the Historic Society of Lancashire and Cheshire*, vol. lxxxviii.
—— 'Hale Hall Glass', in ibid., vol. lxxxix.
—— 'The Ancient Painted Glass from Hale Hall', in ibid., vol. xc.
—— 'The Fifteenth-Century Glass in the Church of St. Michael, Ashton-under-Lyne', in *Archaeological Journal*, vol. lxx.
PANOFSKY, E., *Abbot Suger on the Abbey Church of St. Denis and its Art Treasures*. Princeton, 1946.
PITCHER, S. A., 'Ancient Stained Glass in Gloucestershire Churches', in *Transactions of the Bristol and Gloucestershire Archaeological Society*, vol. xlvii.
RACKHAM, B., *The Ancient Glass of Canterbury Cathedral*. London, 1949.
—— *Victoria and Albert Museum, Department of Ceramics: a Guide to the Collections of Stained Glass*. London, 1936.

RACKHAM, B., 'The Ancient Windows of Christ's College Chapel, Cambridge', in *Archaeological Journal*, vol. cix.

READ, H., *English Stained Glass*. London, 1926.

RIDGWAY, M. H., 'Coloured Window Glass in Cheshire, XIV Century–1550', in *Transactions of the Lancashire and Cheshire Antiquarian Society*, vols. lix–lx.

RUSHFORTH, G. Mc.N., 'An Account of Some Painted Glass from a House at Leicester', in *Archaeological Journal*, vol. lxxv.

—— *Medieval Christian Imagery as illustrated by the Painted Windows of Great Malvern Priory Church, Worcestershire, together with a description and explanation of all the Ancient Glass in the Church*. Oxford, 1936.

—— 'Seven Sacraments Compositions in English Medieval Art', in *Antiquaries Journal*, vol. ix.

—— 'The Great East Window of Gloucester Cathedral', in *Transactions of the Bristol and Gloucestershire Archaeological Society*, vol. xliv.

—— 'The Glass in the Quire Clerestory of Tewkesbury Abbey', in ibid., vol. xlvi.

—— 'The Windows of the Church of St. Neot, Cornwall', in *Transactions of the Exeter Diocesan Architectural and Archaeological Society*, vol. xv.

STEINBERG, S. H., 'A Portrait of Beatrix of Falkenburg', in *Antiquaries Journal*, vol. xviii.

TOKE, N. E., 'The Medieval Stained Glass Windows at Upper Hardres', in *Archaeologia Cantiana*, vol. xlvii.

WINSTON, C., *Memoirs illustrative of the Art of Glass-painting*. London, 1865.

WOODFORDE, C., 'Some Medieval English Glazing Quarries painted with Birds', in *Journal of the British Archaeological Association*, Third Series, vol. ix.

—— *Stained Glass in Somerset, 1250–1830*. London, 1946.

—— *The Norwich School of Glass-Painting in the Fifteenth Century*. London, 1950.

—— 'The Painted Glass in Withcote Church', in *Burlington Magazine*, vol. lxxv, no. cdxxxvi.

—— 'The Stained and Painted Glass in Hengrave Hall, Suffolk', in *Proceedings of the Suffolk Institute of Archaeology and Natural History*, vol. xxii.

—— *The Stained Glass of New College, Oxford*. London, 1951.

COUNTY LIST OF PLACES CONTAINING STAINED GLASS MENTIONED AND ILLUSTRATED IN THIS BOOK

Roman numerals indicate the date of the glass. Arabic numerals indicate the page references. References in black type are to plates

BEDFORDSHIRE
Edworth, XIV, 17.
Eyworth, XV, 27.

BERKSHIRE
Aldermaston, XIII, 3, XVI, 33.
Bradfield College, XIX, 60.
Bucklebury, XVII, 48, **54.**
Childrey, XV, 24.
Eton College, XX, **79.**
Ockwells Manor, XV, 28.
Stanford-in-the-Vale, XIV, 14.
Stratfield Mortimer
St. John, XIX, 60.
St. Mary, XIX, 58.
Wellington College, XX, **80.**

BRISTOL, XIV, 13.

BUCKINGHAMSHIRE
Bradenham, XVI, 33, XVIII, 52, **58.**
Chetwode, XIII, 6.
Hillesden, XVI, 34, 35.
Horton, XIX, 59.
Monks Risborough, XV, 26.
Stoke Poges, XVII, 46, **53.**
Turville, XVIII, 52, **58.**
Whitchurch, XIV, 15.

CAMBRIDGESHIRE
Balsham, XX, 63.
Cambridge
Christ's College, XV–XVI, 30.
King's College, XVI, 33, 35–36, **frontispiece, 43,** XIX, 57.
Peterhouse, XVII, 43–44.
Trinity College, XVIII, 50, **61.**

LIST OF PLACES CONTAINING STAINED GLASS

INDEX

References in black type are to plates

CANTERBURY CATHEDRAL

West Window of the Nave. Adam. *c.* 1178

CANTERBURY CATHEDRAL

South-west Transept. Lamech. *c.* 1178

BRABOURNE, KENT
Grisaille. 12th century

STANTON HARCOURT, OXON.
Grisaille and Panel Window. First half of the 13th century

CANTERBURY CATHEDRAL

North Choir Aisle Triforium. Massacre of the Monks by the Danes. *c.* 1200

CANTERBURY CATHEDRAL

Trinity Chapel. The Story of Eilward of Westoning from one of the 'St. Thomas Becket' Windows. *c.* 1220–5

MADLEY, HEREFORD

East Window. 13th century and later

SALISBURY CATHEDRAL
Panels from Grisaille Windows. 13th century

MERTON COLLEGE, OXFORD

St. Stephen. *c.* 1298–1311

MERTON COLLEGE, OXFORD

Royal Arms and Arms of Clare. *c.* 1298–1311

9

YORK MINSTER
North Aisle of the Nave
Panel from the 'Penancer's' Window. *c.* 1315–20

YORK MINSTER

North Aisle of the Nave. Grisaille. *c.* 1315

BREDON, WORCS.

Grisaille and Panel Window. Early 14th century

WELLS CATHEDRAL

South Aisle of the Choir. Crucifix with Donor. *c.* 1320–5

TEWKESBURY ABBEY, GLOS.

King Solomon. The Prophet Joel. *c.* 1340–4

EATON BISHOP, HEREFORD

St. Michael Weighing a Soul. Early 14th century

YORK MINSTER

South Aisle of the Nave. Joachim in the Wilderness of Sheep. *c.* 1335–50

WARNDON, WORCS.

FLADBURY, WORCS.

The Blessed Virgin Mary and Child. First half of the 14th century

DEERHURST, GLOS.

St. Catherine. Early 14th century

GLOUCESTER CATHEDRAL

East Window. The Blessed Virgin Mary. *c.* 1350

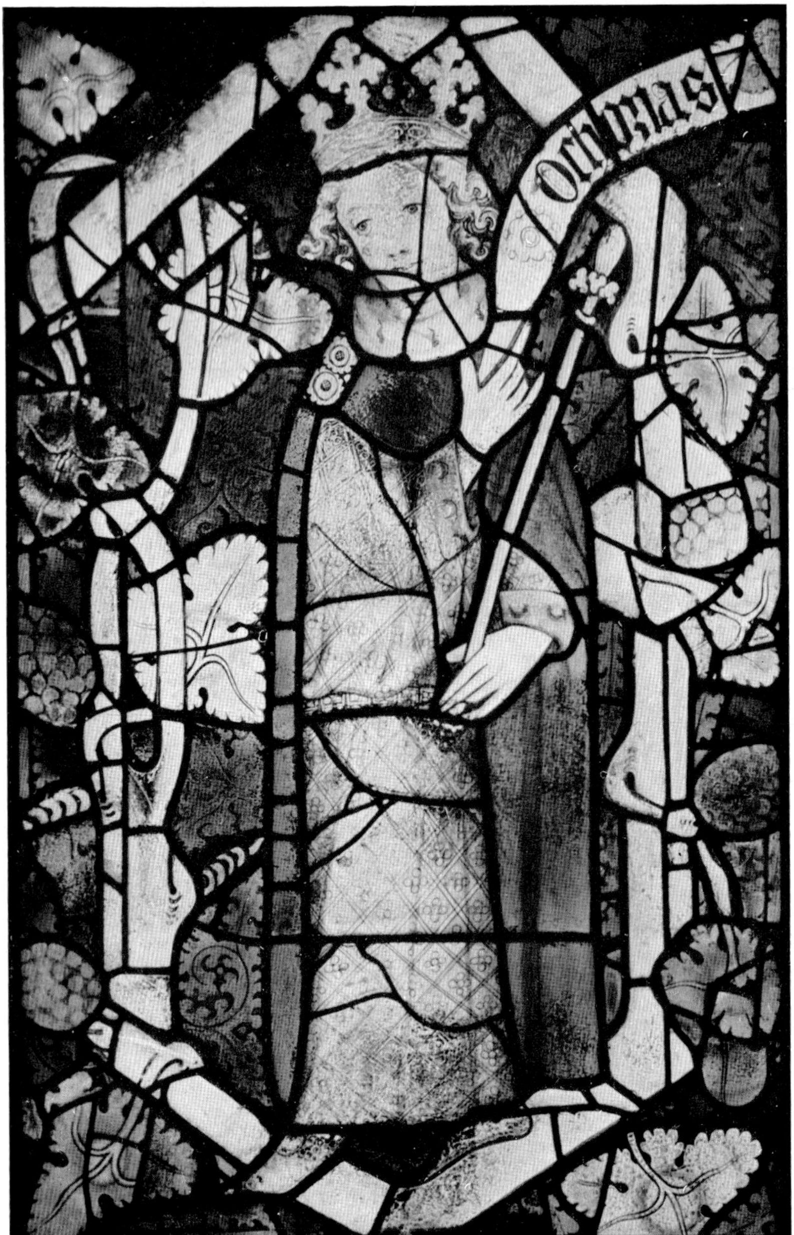

WINCHESTER COLLEGE

Figure of Hezekiah from the Tree of Jesse. *c.* 1393

WINCHESTER COLLEGE

Head of the Blessed Virgin Mary. *c.* 1393

YORK MINSTER

Great East Window. The Angels Holding the Four Winds, from the Apocalypse. By John Thornton of Coventry. 1405–8

YORK MINSTER

Head of St. William from the 'St. William' Window. *c.* 1422

ST. MARTIN, CONEY STREET, YORK

Scene in the Life of St. Martin. *c.* 1432–7

GREAT MALVERN PRIORY

East Window. The Triumphal Entry of Christ into Jerusalem. *c.* 1440

GREAT MALVERN PRIORY

North Clerestory of the Choir. St. Werstan's Vision of the Consecration of his Chapel by Angels. *c.* 1460–70

THE BEAUCHAMP CHAPEL, WARWICK

St. Thomas Becket. St. Alban. By John Prudde. *c.* 1447

COLLEGE OF ST. MARK, AUDLEY END, ESSEX

Quarries. 15th century and later

VICTORIA AND ALBERT MUSEUM
'October.' From Cassiobury Park, Herts.
First half of the 15th century

LEICESTER MUSEUM
The Birth of the Blessed Virgin Mary
Middle of the 15th century

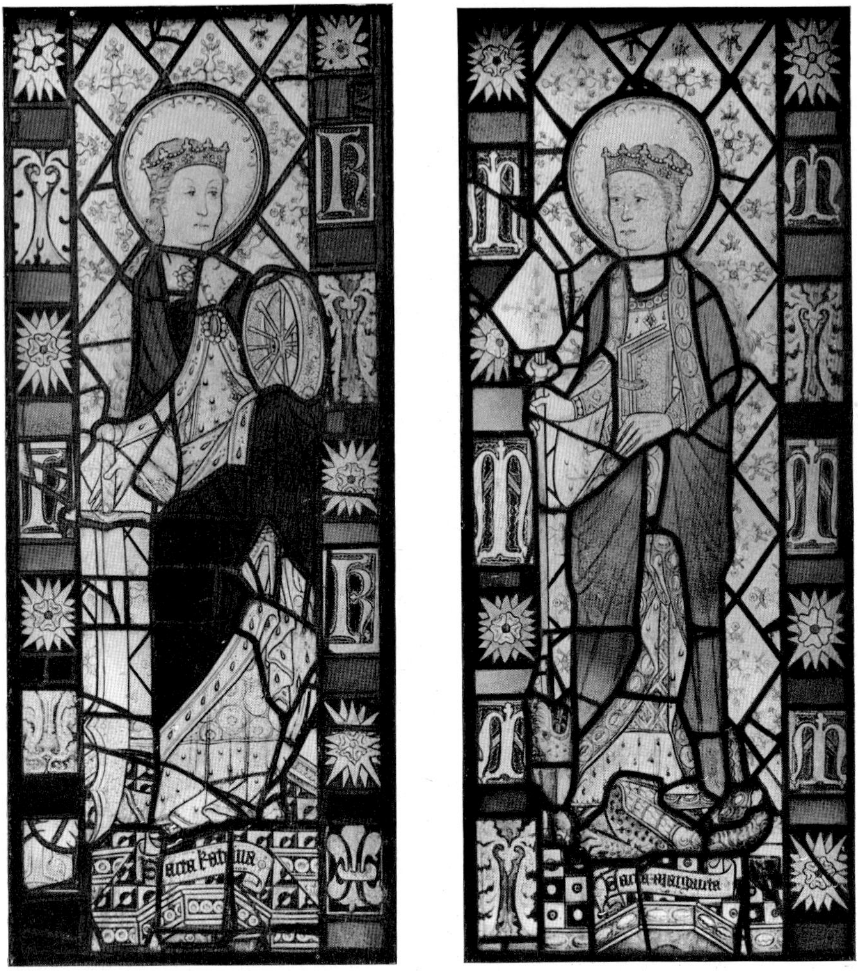

DIDDINGTON, HUNTS.

St. Catherine. St. Margaret. Second half of the 15th century

LONG MELFORD, SUFFOLK

Our Lady of Pity. St. Edmund. Second half of the 15th century

EAST HARLING, NORFOLK

Adoration of the Shepherds. Second half of the 15th century

ALL SAINTS, NORTH STREET, YORK

'Giving Drink to the Thirsty' and 'Visiting the Sick' from the 'Corporal Acts of Mercy' Window. Second half of the 15th century

ALL SAINTS, NORTH STREET, YORK

Two Scenes from the 'Prykke of Conscience' Window

Second half of the 15th century

STRATTON STRAWLESS, NORFOLK

Head of an Angel. Second half of the 15th century

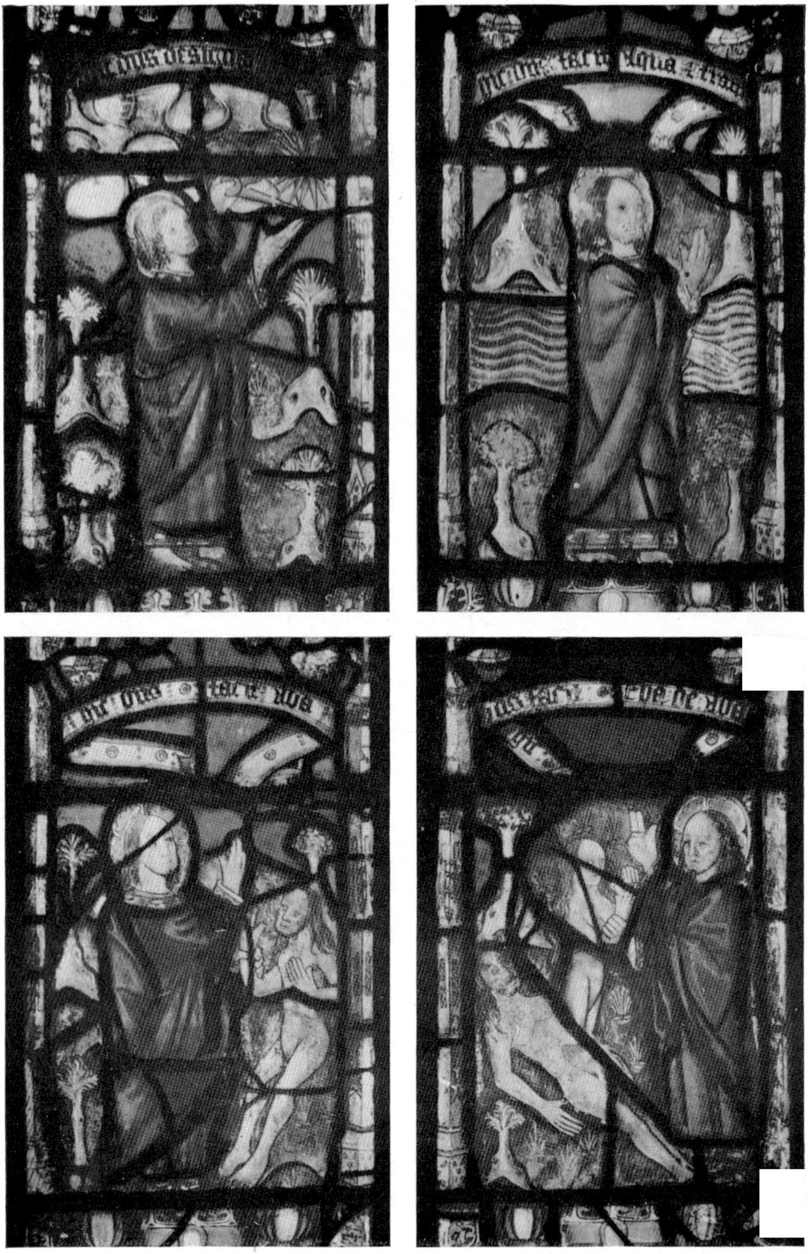

ST. NEOT, CORNWALL

Scenes from the 'Creation' Window. *c.* 1480

36

CANTERBURY CATHEDRAL
North Window of the North-west Transept
Queen Elizabeth Woodville. *c.* 1482

LUDLOW, SALOP

Three Apostles. Late 15th century

VICTORIA AND ALBERT MUSEUM

Crucifixion, with the Blessed Virgin Mary and St. John. From Bramhall Hall, Cheshire. Early 16th century

VICTORIA AND ALBERT MUSEUM

Quarries. From Westminster Abbey and elsewhere
15th and 16th centuries

FAIRFORD, GLOS.

Christ Appearing to the Blessed Virgin Mary after the Resurrection. The Transfiguration. Christ Appearing to the Holy Women after the Resurrection. *c.* 1495–1505

SHELTON, NORFOLK

Anne Shelton. Early 16th century

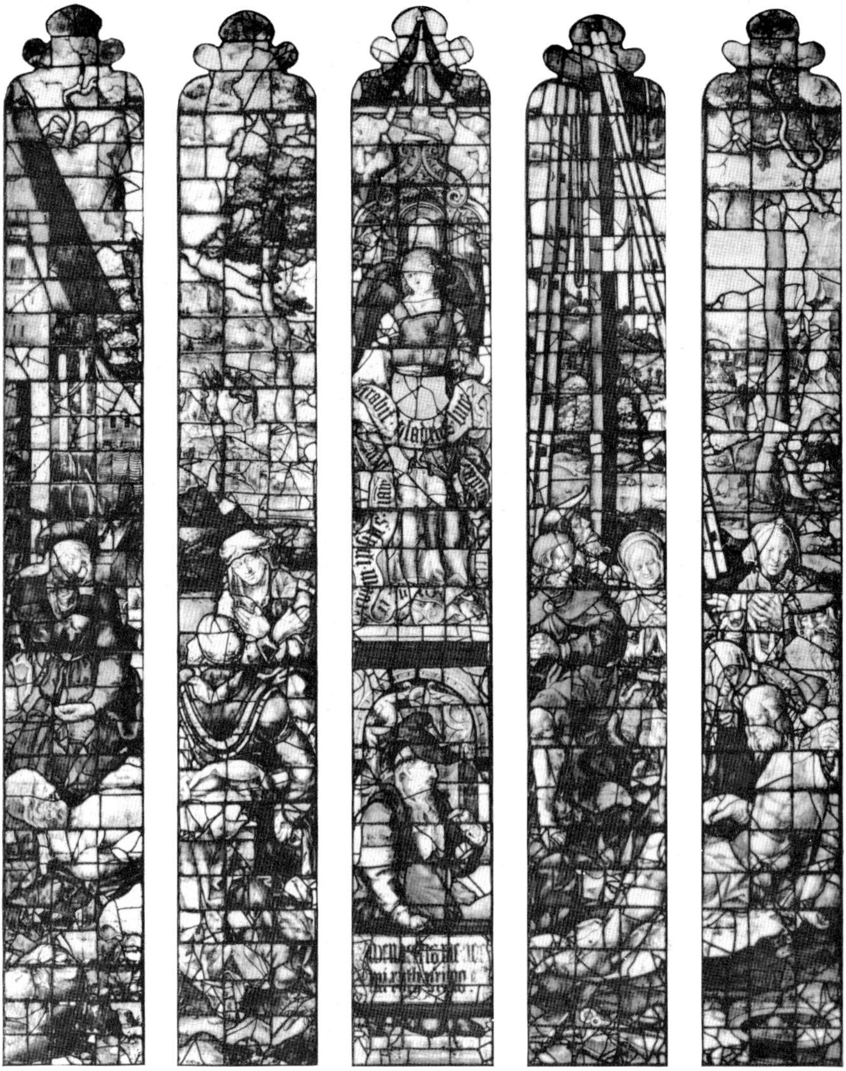

KING'S COLLEGE, CAMBRIDGE

Elimelech Bewailed. Christ Bewailed. *c.* 1526–31

WINSCOMBE, SOMERSET

St. Peter the Apostle. St. Peter the Exorcist. *c.* 1521–32

WITHCOTE, LEICS.
St. Jude. 1537

VICTORIA AND ALBERT MUSEUM

Royal Arms. From Cowick Priory, Devon. *c.* 1540

VICTORIA AND ALBERT MUSEUM

Arms of Lucas. From Filby Hall, Norfolk. 1582

VICTORIA AND ALBERT MUSEUM
Arms of Pigott quartering Castelline and Walcott. 1562

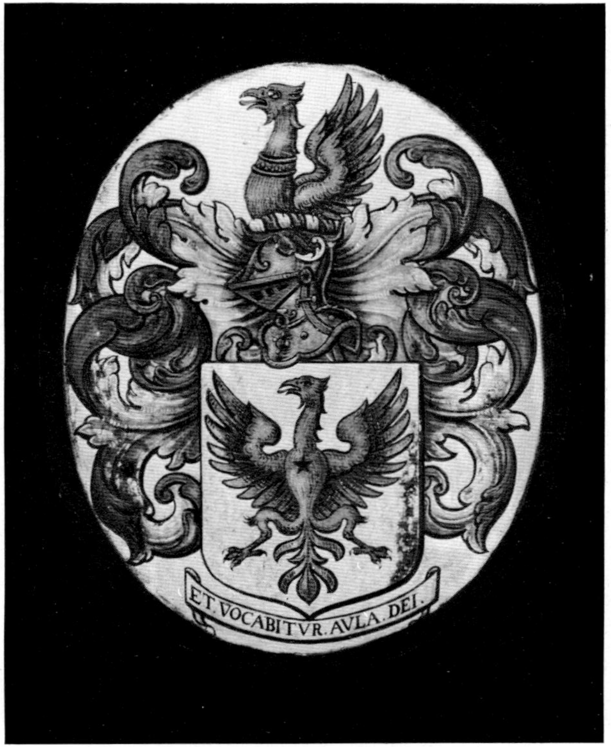

SOUTH NEWINGTON, OXON.
Achievement of Hall. Early 17th century

VICTORIA AND ALBERT MUSEUM

Quarries and Medallions. From Preston Hall, Suffolk. *c.* 1600

CHRIST CHURCH, OXFORD

Jonah before Nineveh. By Abraham van Linge. *c.* 1630–40

MAGDALEN COLLEGE, OXFORD

King Charles I and his Queen. By Richard Greenbury. 1633

BARNINGHAM WINTER, NORFOLK

Royal Arms. *Temp.* Charles I

STOKE POGES, BUCKS.

Arms of Ducie impaling Pipe and Ducie impaling Pigott. Middle of the 17th century

BUCKLEBURY, BERKS.
Sundial. 1649

STAVELEY, DERBY.
Window by Henry Gyles. 1676

LOW HAM, SOMERSET

East Window. *c.* 1690

HERTFORD MUSEUM

Panel dated 1701

BRADENHAM, BUCKS.
Arms of Martha Lovelace, Baroness Wentworth. 18th century

TURVILLE, BUCKS.
Arms of Sidney quarterly of twenty-eight *c.* 1733

GREAT WITLEY, WORCS.
Adoration of the Kings. By Joshua Price. 1719

THE VYNE, HANTS

Adoration of the Shepherds. By John Rowell the younger. 1770

TRINITY COLLEGE, CAMBRIDGE

Alma Mater Presenting Isaac Newton to King George III. Designed by Giovanni Battista Cipriani and painted by William Peckitt. 1775

AUDLEY END, ESSEX

Head of Christ from the 'Last Supper'. Designed by Biagio Rebecca and painted by William Peckitt. 1771

NEW COLLEGE, OXFORD

'Fortitude' and 'Justice'. Designed by Sir Joshua Reynolds and painted by Thomas Jervais. 1778

DUDLEY, WORCS.

The Resurrection. By Joseph Backler. 1821

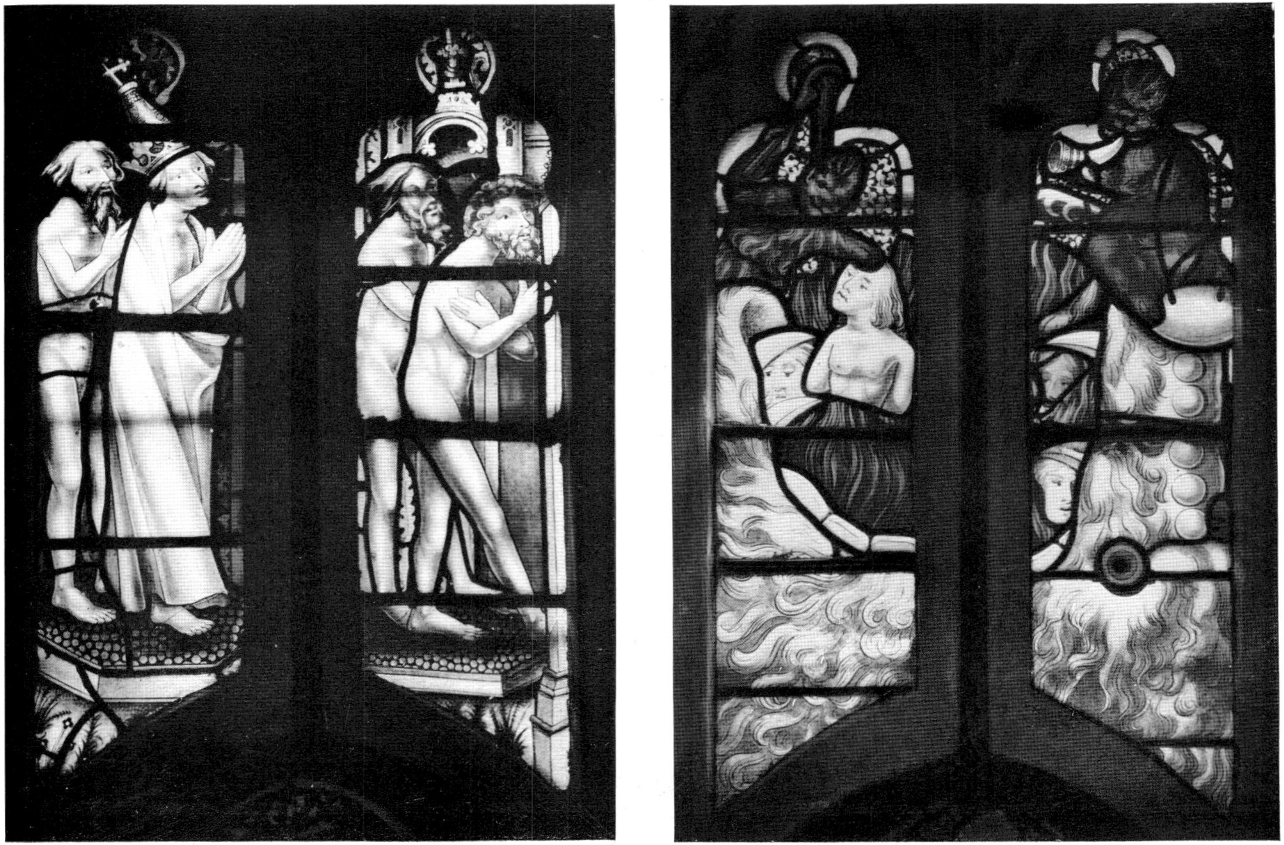

WINCHESTER COLLEGE

The Blessed and the Damned. Copy of 14th-century glass. By John Betton and David Evans. 1822

BROCKLEY, SOMERSET

Window by W. R. Eginton. *c.* 1824–9

BURY ST. EDMUNDS CATHEDRAL
East Window. By John Hardman and Co. 1868

WIMPOLE, CAMBS.

Memorial Window to Victor Alexander Yorke. *c.* 1868

BARDWELL, SUFFOLK

Window by O'Connor. 1869

WIGHTWICK MANOR, WOLVERHAMPTON
Summer. By C. E. Kempe. 1874

GREAT MALVERN PRIORY

Panel from 1887 Jubilee Window. By Messrs. Winfield Ltd.

BIRMINGHAM CATHEDRAL

The Last Judgement. By Edward Burne-Jones. 1897

ASHBOURNE, DERBY

Window by Christopher Whall. *c.* 1901

WINCHELSEA, SUSSEX

Window by Douglas Strachan. 1929

CHURCH OF THE ASCENSION, BITTERNE PARK, SOUTHAMPTON

Window by A. K. Nicholson and G. E. R. Smith. 1930

THORPE, DERBY

Window by F. C. Eden. 1930

CHICHESTER CATHEDRAL

Lights from Windows in the North Aisle. By Christopher Webb. 1949

ST. STEPHEN'S PORCH, WESTMINSTER HALL

Heraldic Glass. Ninian Comper. 1952

ETON COLLEGE
Window by Evie Hone. 1952

WELLINGTON COLLEGE

Windows by Hugh Easton. 1952